Blended Families

Other Books in the Social Issues Firsthand Series:

AIDS

Bullying

Child Abuse and Neglect

Cliques

Date and Acquaintance Rape

Disasters

Drunk Driving

Eating Disorders

Juvenile Crime

Mixed Heritage

Prostitution

Sexual Predators

Teenage Pregnancy

Web 2.0

Blended Families

Stefan Kiesbye, Book Editor

GREENHAVEN PRESS
A part of Gale, Cengage Learning

Detroit • New York • San Francisco • New Haven, Conn • Waterville, Maine • London

Christine Nasso, *Publisher*
Elizabeth Des Chenes, *Managing Editor*

For more information, contact:
Greenhaven Press
27500 Drake Rd.
Farmington Hills, MI 48331-3535
Or you can visit our Internet site at gale.cengage.com

Articles in Greenhaven Press anthologies are often edited for length to meet page requirements. In addition, original titles of these works are changed to clearly present the main thesis and to explicitly indicate the author's opinion. Every effort is made to ensure that Greenhaven Press accurately reflects the original intent of the authors. Every effort has been made to trace the owners of copyrighted material.

LIBRARY OF CONGRESS CATALOGING-IN-PUBLICATION DATA

Blended families / Stefan Kiesbye, editor.
p. cm. -- (Social issues firsthand)
Includes bibliographical references and index.
ISBN 978-0-7377-4559-7 (hardcover)
1. Stepfamilies--United States. I. Kiesbye, Stefan.
HQ759.92.B545 2009
306.874'70973--dc22

2009008627

Printed in the United States of America
1 2 3 4 5 6 7 13 12 11 10 09

Contents

Foreword 9

Introduction 12

Chapter 1: Growing Up in a Blended Family

1. A Stepbrother Becomes a Brother 17

   Lyssa Friedman

   The author recounts the many difficulties she faced growing up in a blended family, but also the strong bond she formed with her stepbrother. As children they grew to understand each other's confusion, and they were able to carry their mutual love into adulthood.

2. Another Mother's Love 21

   Heidi Bernadette Mack

   In this essay, the writer relates how, when her natural mother passed away, she accepted her new stepmother as a part of her family and her life. New routines became a part of everyday life for the author and her sister, making it even easier to begin creating new and happier memories.

3. I Was Stressed by the Fights of My Blended Family 24

   Kathryn Esplin

   When she is twelve years old, the author's father gets remarried to a Polish scientist. Torn from her Mormon community, and hardly able to communicate with her stepbrother and stepmother, she grows to hate the woman she initially adored and finds herself unable to fit in.

4. My Father's Mysterious New Life 31

   Michelle Lupton

   As a child, the author idolizes her father's new wife, a beautiful and exotic-looking woman, and is heartbroken when the couple leaves for remote Pitcairn Island. Years later she visits and revises the dreamed-up pictures of island life, and gains new respect for her father's family.

5. The Man I Call "Dad" Is the Man Who Raised Me **36**

Marc Lynott

Even though his biological father remained a presence in his life, the writer learns over the years to call his stepfather "Dad." But he finds that his choice to finally spend Father's Day with the man who raised him and not with the man who brought him into the world is not an easy one to live with.

6. My Real Father Is Not My Dad **41**

Sarah Ivens

Growing up without her biological father, the writer develops close ties to her stepdad and is thankful for getting a second chance at family life. Whenever her real father wants to claim her as his daughter, to impress visitors or friends, she remembers that he was not the one who raised her, and she does not feel any special ties to him anymore.

Chapter 2: Parenting in Blended Families

1. Most Families Do Not Blend **49**

Ron Deal, interviewed by Duane Careb and Jim Mueller

Ron Deal, who runs a seminar on stepfamilies, talks about the challenges of new relationships that are not quite equal, about the risks parents take when children do not approve of a new partner, and about how stepparents can work smarter instead of harder.

2. The Real Lives of Blended Families Do Not Follow TV Scripts **55**

Jennifer Busse McClenon

Informed about blended families mainly by TV's *The Brady Bunch*, the author has a rude awakening when starting to care for her own. She has to let go of the cute images and lower the bar on expectations to become a successful stepmom.

3. Bringing Together Parents and Stepparents 59

Lisa Cohn

Despite the potential for ugly arguments, the author invites her ex-husband and her new husband's ex-wife to her house to have dinner together. After many awkward moments the families finally come together as one.

4. A Different Kind of Mother's Day 64

Dawn Miller

Mother's Day can be awkward, the author finds out, when you are not the biological mother of the children you are raising. There are hardly any greeting cards for stepmothers, and teachers do not encourage their students to craft gifts for their stepparents. Yet after years of feeling on the outside, she finds that her stepdaughter has not forgotten the occasion.

5. Stepfamilies Are Normal Families 67

Laurie McGough Hanson

Having been a stepdaughter and stepsister herself, the author expects to have few problems when she marries a divorced man with children. She is wrong, but despite the struggles, her new family grows strong ties and overcomes the many initial gaps.

Chapter 3: Toward a New Understanding of Family

1. Leaving Behind Traditional Views of Belonging 73

Natasha Sky

Single-parent families, two-mom, two-dad, and blended families challenge society's traditional images of what family means. But in many schoolbooks, the author observes, the new families are still absent, as if years of change have gone unnoticed, and she argues for texts and learning materials that reflect modern diversity.

2. Growing Up in a Group Marriage 77
Laird Harrison
At the age of nine, the writer's parents move in with another married couple and their children. What started as a summer love-relationship becomes an experiment in group marriage. And even though the blended family does not survive, Harrison mourns the loss of a special kind of camaraderie.

3. Divorce Does Not Have to Be the End of Family 81
Constance Ahrons
While attending the wedding of her "ex-husband's daughter by his second wife," the author reflects on divorce and how family break-ups can lead to new togetherness, enlarging and enriching family rather than impoverishing it.

4. Blending Families and Faiths 86
Barbara Miksch
The author writes about her positive experience not only creating a blended family by getting remarried, but also bringing together different faiths for all members to share.

5. A Marriage Blending Family and Race 90
Bill Grady
Having four white and four biracial children and a host of grandchildren, Bill Grady talks about overcoming stereotypes, threats to his family because of skin color, and the possibility of building families that defy tradition.

Organizations to Contact 94

For Further Research 97

Index 101

Foreword

Social issues are often viewed in abstract terms. Pressing challenges such as poverty, homelessness, and addiction are viewed as problems to be defined and solved. Politicians, social scientists, and other experts engage in debates about the extent of the problems, their causes, and how best to remedy them. Often overlooked in these discussions is the human dimension of the issue. Behind every policy debate over poverty, homelessness, and substance abuse, for example, are real people struggling to make ends meet, to survive life on the streets, and to overcome addiction to drugs and alcohol. Their stories are ubiquitous and compelling. They are the stories of everyday people—perhaps your own family members or friends—and yet they rarely influence the debates taking place in state capitols, the national Congress, or the courts.

The disparity between the public debate and private experience of social issues is well illustrated by looking at the topic of poverty. Each year the U.S. Census Bureau establishes a poverty threshold. A household with an income below the threshold is defined as poor, while a household with an income above the threshold is considered able to live on a basic subsistence level. For example, in 2003 a family of two was considered poor if its income was less than $12,015; a family of four was defined as poor if its income was less than $18,810. Based on this system, the bureau estimates that 35.9 million Americans (12.5 percent of the population) lived below the poverty line in 2003, including 12.9 million children below the age of eighteen.

Commentators disagree about what these statistics mean. Social activists insist that the huge number of officially poor Americans translates into human suffering. Even many families that have incomes above the threshold, they maintain, are likely to be struggling to get by. Other commentators insist that the statistics exaggerate the problem of poverty in the United States. Compared to people in developing countries, they point out, most so-called poor families have a high quality of life. As stated by journalist Fidelis Iyebote, "Cars are owned by 70 percent of 'poor' households. . . . Color televisions belong to 97 percent of the 'poor' [and] videocassette recorders belong to nearly 75 percent. . . . Sixty-four percent have microwave ovens, half own a stereo system, and over a quarter possess an automatic dishwasher."

However, this debate over the poverty threshold and what it means is likely irrelevant to a person living in poverty. Simply put, poor people do not need the government to tell them whether they are poor. They can see it in the stack of bills they cannot pay. They are aware of it when they are forced to choose between paying rent or buying food for their children. They become painfully conscious of it when they lose their homes and are forced to live in their cars or on the streets. Indeed, the written stories of poor people define the meaning of poverty more vividly than a government bureaucracy could ever hope to. Narratives composed by the poor describe losing jobs due to injury or mental illness, depict horrific tales of childhood abuse and spousal violence, recount the loss of friends and family members. They evoke the slipping away of social supports and government assistance, the descent into substance abuse and addiction, the harsh realities of life on the streets. These are the perspectives on poverty that are too often omitted from discussions over the extent of the problem and how to solve it.

Greenhaven Press's *Social Issues Firsthand* series provides a forum for the often-overlooked human perspectives on society's most divisive topics of debate. Each volume focuses on one social issue and presents a collection of ten to sixteen narratives by those who have had personal involvement with the topic. Extra care has been taken to include a diverse range of perspectives. For example, in the volume on adoption, readers will find the stories of birth parents who have made an adoption plan, adoptive parents, and adoptees themselves. After exposure to these varied points of view, the reader will have a clearer understanding that adoption is an intense, emotional experience full of joyous highs and painful lows for all concerned.

The debate surrounding embryonic stem cell research illustrates the moral and ethical pressure that the public brings to bear on the scientific community. However, while nonexperts often criticize scientists for not considering the potential negative impact of their work, ironically the public's reaction against such discoveries can produce harmful results as well. For example, although the outcry against embryonic stem cell research in the United States has resulted in fewer embryos being destroyed, those with Parkinson's, such as actor Michael J. Fox, have argued that prohibiting the development of new stem cell lines ultimately will prevent a timely cure for the disease that is killing Fox and thousands of others.

Each book in the series contains several features that enhance its usefulness, including an in-depth introduction, an annotated table of contents, bibliographies for further research, a list of organizations to contact, and a thorough index. These elements—combined with the poignant voices of people touched by tragedy and triumph—make the Social Issues Firsthand series a valuable resource for research on today's topics of political discussion.

Introduction

"In the catalog of family values," acclaimed author Barbara Kingsolver writes,

> where do we rank an occasion like this? A curly-haired boy who wanted to run before he walked, age seven now, a soccer player scoring a winning goal. He turns to the bleachers with his fists in the air and a smile wide as a gap-toothed galaxy. His own cheering section of grown-ups and kids all leap to their feet and hug each other, delirious with love for this boy. He's Andy, my best friend's son. The cheering section includes his mother and her friends, his brother, his father and stepmother, a stepbrother and stepsister, and a grandparent. Lucky is the child with this many relatives on hand to hail a proud accomplishment. I'm there too, witnessing a family fortune. But in spite of myself, defensive words take shape in my head. I am thinking: I dare *anybody* to call this a broken home.

When people talk about family, what type of family do they imagine in their heads? Is it the two parents, two children (a boy and a girl, of course) of so many schoolbooks and TV shows, or does it have a different look?

With the divorce rate in America hovering around 40 to 50 percent, the traditional family is not the only model, and may not even be the dominant one anymore. The U.S. Department of Health and Human Services estimates that "by the age of 18, over 20 percent of American children will experience the divorce of their parents." The American Blended Family Association (ABFA) recently

> distributed an "Open Letter to the 2008 [Presidential] Candidates" for the purpose of placing into the national political debate a unique set of governing issues impacting this growing demographic.... Research shows that during the

term of the next U.S. President, blended family households will become the most common form of family residence in America. More Americans are part of step-family situations today—over 110 million people—than voted in the last presidential election.

An early example of a blended family was *The Brady Bunch*, TV's bright group of shiny individuals with happy problems. While *The Brady Bunch* did a lot to make blended families socially acceptable and remove the stigma of divorce and remarriage, it didn't do justice to the complex challenges of real blended families. Psychologist Daniel Kaeck writes, "Blended families appear not to work—the Brady Bunch is bunk. Today, over 70% of mothers of preschoolers use alternative childcare, i.e. are employed full-time. Fewer families have meals together; adults spend 6 hours shopping per week and only 40 minutes solely with their children." And many adults have a hard time adjusting to marrying a family. Journalist Sandy Sims reports that

> for Norbert Fronczak and his wife, Margaret, having a stepfamily meant a long, painful learning curve and a major test of their relationship. Norbert thought stepfamily problems would simply work themselves out when he and Margaret married seven years ago. His two sons were 3 and 7. Margaret had been married before but had no children. As an African American marrying a Caucasian, she wasn't concerned about mixed-race issues, but she'd read books about stepfamilies and knew trouble was ahead. "I cried," she said, "but I was very much in love with this man and wanted to marry him."

The reality, unlike the TV show, is often brutal. Sims explains:

> New stepparents, ex-spouses and the children are rarely prepared for what's ahead. Dr. Don Partridge, Ph.D., president of the Institute for Family Research and Education . . . , and his wife, Jenetha, . . . have been stepparents to seven children

> for some 20 years. Partridge used the metaphor "extreme environment" to describe . . . what a stepfamily is about. "Things become dangerous and difficult fast," Partridge says. "You have to be prepared."

In Partridge's estimate, more than 60 percent of blended families fail.

The victims of troubled blended families are often the children. Dan Snell, CEO of ABFA, states that "people don't enter into marriage ever thinking they will fail, and have to start over again. Yet if they do, the dynamics, especially when children are involved, can be life shocking." In a research paper, scholars Donna Ginther and Robert Pollak find that children in blended families are at a disadvantage when it comes to education. "We find that children reared in traditional nuclear families . . . have substantially better outcomes than the joint biological children from stable blended families. Within stable blended families we find that the difference between the joint biological children and the stepchildren is neither substantial nor statistically significant."

Trying to blend families is stressful, and stress may be the biggest reason why children in blended families perform less well. And society may not be helping. Kingsolver states that "there's a current in the air with ferocious moral force that finds its way even into political campaigns, claiming there is only one right way to do it, the Way It Has Always Been. In the face of a thriving, particolored world, this narrow view is so pickled and absurd I'm astonished that it gets airplay. And I'm astonished that it still stings."

While blending families will never look like an episode of *The Brady Bunch*, society can help ease the pains of the endeavor. Whether people approve of divorce and remarriage or not, whether they approve of blended families or not—divorce is a reality, and it will help children and parents in blended families to reduce anxiety and stress if society offers a help and understanding. To remove social stigma will be of great importance. "To protect family life, children, marriage, and single parents, we believe that our elected leaders must act to support and strengthen the family," says Dan Snell. And to an ever larger degree, the U.S. family will be blended.

Chapter 1

Growing Up in a Blended Family

A Stepbrother Becomes a Brother

Lyssa Friedman

Thrown together into one household, the author slowly starts bonding with her stepbrother Phil. They share interests, as well as a sense of responsibility for the new home, and their mutual respect and compassion carry over into adulthood. Lyssa Friedman is an award-winning writer whose work has appeared in The Christian Science Monitor *and* San Francisco Chronicle.

I rolled my new pre-owned car home from the lot and phoned my stepbrother Phil in Nevada. "I'm getting rid of the Civic," I told him. "It's yours."

Phil drove an Accord whose odometer had rolled over twice. I figured he could use reliable wheels that had traveled only 100,000 miles. "No thanks," he said. "My Honda's running fine."

"Phil," I persisted, "you don't have to buy it. It's a gift. I owe you a vehicle."

I took Phil back to the dealer-plated '74 Dodge pickup he bought the year before we graduated from our Massachusetts high school. My mother had married his dad not long before, and had moved her three children in with his four. In a house with seven kids, thrift was king, and cars were purchased used, never new. The town was semirural then, and it was as common for teenagers to have their own cars as it was to pose for a yearbook picture.

We stepkids' ages overlapped, so most of us attended high school at the same time, which meant that our driveway was a jumble of rusty station wagons parked next to teen-envy vans with shag-carpeted interiors. My stepfather's agreement to co-

Lyssa Friedman, "The Debt I Owe Is the Gift We Share," *Christian Science Monitor*, April 26, 2001. Reproduced by permission.

sign Phil's new car loan, representing a departure from family culture, demonstrated faith in Phil and his future.

In 1977, Phil got behind the wheel of that future, drove the Dodge west, and found a permanent parking spot in Nevada. The next year I followed and settled in San Francisco. Every few months he took the pickup to the Bay Area to visit me.

"Don't you remember what happened?" I reminded Phil now.

Wrecking Her Stepbrother's Car

During one of those visits, he loaned me the truck. While I cruised at 55 m.p.h. in Interstate 80's slow lane, a flatbed pulled in front of me from a shoulder stop. I skidded, rear-ended the flatbed, and spun 360 degrees, wrecking Phil's pickup.

"That was long ago," Phil said. "You do not owe me a car."

"Yes, I owe you," I thought. "No way I'll accept your refusal."

Before my mother married Phil's dad, the only stepfamily our parents knew was *The Brady Bunch*. On television, conflicts were resolved in 30 minutes, minus commercials. Bunk beds blend a family, the newlyweds decided.

Meanwhile, we stepchildren circled each other like cats, trying to adjust to a marriage we hadn't chosen. Yes, we doubled up in bedrooms. But we functioned like seven only children tossed together rather than one unified family.

Phil and I were the independent, well-behaved middle children. We showed up for school, turned in homework. We got our chores done and came home on time. I baked double batches of Toll House cookies. Phil mowed the lawn. We avoided activities that would call attention to us.

Then one day, after Phil finished raking, he joined me in the kitchen, where he nibbled steaming cookies and gulped milk. "Mmm, good. Thanks," he said, lingering.

Baking was my job, and thanks were a surprise. I expected Phil to grab a snack and hide in his bedroom with the stereo cranked, not keep me company and throw in a compliment. We became buddies.

He had a motorcycle that he seemed to disembowel once a month, diagnosing a problem only he could detect, then reassembling it bit by greasy bit. On summer afternons, I sat and watched.

After he kick-started it, I'd put on the second helmet and climb behind, leaning with him into the curves as we cooled ourselves in the wind's air conditioning.

When he traded the motorbike for the pickup, I helped him buff it to a high shine. We pulled on cutoffs, loaded a rowboat and a cooler in the back, and drove to the nearby lake. We took turns pulling oars.

Getting to Know Each Other

At the lake's center, where the depth turned the water ebony, we dove in and floated on our backs, gazing at the lazy sky.

Phil and I never talked about what drew us together, but we had plenty in common. We'd each lost a parent and we stifled our feelings, even from ourselves. We moved cheerily into our parents' second marriage. Then, at the eye of our unwieldy clan's cyclone, we blended into the background.

Although neither of us could express losses deeper than that summer lake's center, I think now that we understood each other. Phil reached toward me when I didn't know I was sinking. And instead of diving in to contemplate the water's bottomless darkness, I resurfaced and found a friend splashing beside me. Our companionship assured us, gently, that we would survive.

Now I offered Phil a car and he refused. How would I compensate him for the demolished vehicle?

I thought back to the phone call when I told Phil I'd totaled his treasured truck. "Phil, I have bad news. I had an accident."

He sucked in a breath. "Were you hurt?"

"Phil, the truck's totaled."

"I asked, were you hurt?"

"No."

"That's all that matters," he said.

And I realized that crashing Phil's pick-up didn't put me in his debt. His love for me did. Giving him a car wouldn't even my balance sheet. I'd owe Phil for the rest of my life. And this was an obligation that, finally, I would never want to be rid of.

Another Mother's Love

Heidi Bernadette Mack

The author's natural mother passed away when she was only eight years old. Her father remarried some time after, and the author found it easy to accept her stepmother as a part of her family and her life. Hearty breakfasts and new routines became a part of everyday life for the author and her sister, making it even easier for her to accept her new mother, and even to begin creating new and happier memories.

Not all stepfamilies have to struggle as they work toward love and unity. My own experience was happy from the beginning. I'm sure my natural mother loved me, and I her, even though I don't remember her very well. I was 8 and my sister was 12 when our mother passed on.

But we didn't have the mother–daughter closeness apparent in some families. I don't remember listening to bedtime stories while being tucked gently beneath the covers or while cuddling on her lap, her cool hands stroking my hair.

Ready For a New Mother

When my father announced his plans to remarry a number of months later, I was surprised, but not unhappy.

I still remember where we were and where we had eaten dinner, how the gold-flecked diamonds on the seats of my dad's truck felt under my hand as he told us.

Not having spent much time with my natural mother, I was ready to welcome a new mother, who was home when I went to bed at night and got up in the morning.

I don't remember too much from the first few months in our revised family. Some things do stand out—getting over

Heidi Bernadette Mack, "Another Mother's Love: I Call my Stepmother 'Mom,'" *Christian Science Monitor*, November 14, 2008. Reproduced by permission from Christian Science Monitor, (www.csmonitor.com).

the awkwardness of calling a new woman "Mom," the Madame Alexander doll with her yellow dotted dress she brought me, and adjusting to a new schedule—which for the first time included regular bedtime hours and church.

And all the new rules!

Having been used to spending a lot of time on our own, my sister and I weren't used to someone's telling us what to wear, what we could watch on TV, and what to eat.

No more mornings of Pop Tarts and Captain Crunch. We were now awakened to a mother who served us oatmeal and wheat toast.

Days of wearing shorts and flip-flops to school were definitely over. My mother made me some outfits that I hated to wear. I didn't tell her, because I didn't want to hurt her feelings. But they were so out of style—especially the green pantsuit with gold trim!

(Junior high is a place where you just have to fit in, or you'll be cast out forever as a "nerd.")

Natural Adjustments to the "New Mom"

All in all, though, changing a few habits and styles wasn't too much to ask of us, and it didn't take me long to adjust to having a new mother.

I'll never forget the time we were making chocolate chip cookies late one Saturday morning. In my eagerness to taste the batter, I leaned over just a little too far and got my hair tangled in the beaters.

My mom and sister were sure it was the funniest thing they'd ever seen. I did not.

They made me stand, glaring, for a picture with the beater twisted through my brown hair, full of gooey batter.

And the time our dog, Nemo, was killed by a car during a lightning storm. When I came home from school, my mother pulled me onto her lap to comfort me. I was crying uncontrollably. She was completely at a loss as to what to do.

"I'll do anything," she said, "anything, if you'll just stop crying."

"Don't . . . ," I sobbed, stuttering, "make me wear. . .that green pantsuit anymore. . . ."

Poor Nemo was temporarily forgotten. How we laugh about that now!

My sister had a tougher time adjusting than I did, but not really because of the stepmother situation. It was just that hard time of maturing, leaving childhood behind for the new challenges of being a teen-ager.

Looking back, not only did we gain a new mother, we also got a new sister (already married by that time), and lots of wonderful new relatives.

Family Is Family, Regardless of Blood Ties

I cherish this new family situation. It seems foreign to think of my mother and sister as stepmother and stepsister. They're simply family.

It was wonderful, and still is, to have a mother who cared for me as if I were her own. What makes and cements a family, after all, are not merely blood ties.

To me, a real mother is the woman who brings a child up with care, love, and respect—regardless of whether she brought him or her into the world.

I Was Stressed by the Fights of My Blended Family

Kathryn Esplin

When her father gets re-married to a Polish scientist, the author—then twelve years old—initially adores her stepmother. The new couple is devoted to each other, and it seems a match made in heaven. Yet family life brings out the worst in her parents, and the daughter abhors the constant fights. Slowly she learns to fear and loathe her stepmother, until her father's death ends the volatile marriage. Kathryn Esplin is a journalist.

I used to wonder when the world would end. I hoped that it would.

I'm referring to my father's remarriage to my stepmother. It was a nightmare for the entire time between the beginning of the marriage until his death, eight years later.

I've written of my father's life, his death. I've written of my mother's illness, of my stepmother's life. Those were all loving tributes.

I've not told yet of the horrors of living the life after the divorce.

Mental health professionals will tell you that divorce is not as harmful as the effects of a badly structured remarriage. By that, I mean divorce has its own demons for the family, and remarriage has additional demons.

My stepmother was, and is, a Polish woman and a medical doctor, who came from Poland in 1960 specifically to work with my father.

My father was a young scientist at the time, and had an international reputation in his field of pharmacology, the

Kathryn Esplin, "Of Things Human, Life, Remarriage, Death," Gather.com, May, 11, 2006. Reproduced by permission.

study of drugs and their effects upon the central nervous system—in other words, the brain.

My stepmother was a general practitioner in Poland; she had grown up and lived through the Holocaust, a horrible, nearly unspeakable event in her life.

She had one son, a boy one year my senior.

She desired to switch professions and applied for a position as a post-doctoral student, to work directly with my father.

This, the then-Communist Poland granted her. For one year, she would study neuropharmacology, under my father's tutelage.

A New Relationship Begins

From the start, it was a match made in heaven. A 35-year-old, vivacious redhead with a body that wouldn't quit, she had a strong personality that drew people to it like flies to flypaper.

This analogy is apt. She knew well that you draw more flies with honey than with vinegar.

My father had grown up a cowboy, on a ranch in southern Utah, during the depression. Sheep cut the grass during this time. My grandfather's business, a seed and feed store for the sheep industry, failed.

My father was a misfit in this tight-knit Mormon community. As a child, he was wayward. Like many during his time, he started driving a truck when he was 11. He helped drive the truck on the ranch. This all seems so foreign for the 21st century world in which we now live.

My father helped in his father's store; my grandfather had survived mustard gas during World War I in France and could not sweep the fine corn dust off the floor of the store.

So, that became my father's job growing up. How he hated the smell of corn meal and corn bread, that the rest of us so loved.

My father smoked cigarettes from 11 years of age. As I said, this was a small, tight-knit community of Mormons in southern Utah.

Looking for Trouble

You were either part of the religion, or you were outcast. You were either part of the solution, or part of the problem.

No middle ground existed. You could not see beyond the horizon of red mountains in the color country of Southern Utah, affectionately termed "Dixie."

He was sheltered, in spite of this somewhat rough living. He wanted to be a scientist from the age of 10. Going to college was frowned upon, that was for "rich folk," my grandfather had admonished.

After high school, my father joined the U.S. Navy, as World War II was still in progress. The year in training was rough on him, as he was as sensitive as he was sheltered.

It was a lucky moment that he had been born in 1927 and was not called to the military until the end of the war. The war ended just before his training period was over.

He was 19 when he married my mother, his high-school sweetheart. She was 20.

Their wedding photo is of him in his Naval uniform, his dress blues, in San Francisco, where he was stationed.

During this beginning period of his 15-year marriage to my mother, they were at the University of Utah, each getting their bachelor's degree. My father found his métier [vocation or trade]. Science was his "thing."

He had a natural brilliance, a creative force unmatched by many of his contemporaries.

He had scored top in the state in some sort of test that was a pre-cursor to the National Merit Scholarship.

His high school grades were awful; they ranged the gamut. The principal told him that the best thing for him would be to leave high school, never mind he had not completed all his requirements for a diploma. He did not care. He was at the university, courtesy of the G.I. Bill.

He smoked cigarettes; he drank beer and hard liquor. Not to excess, but still, he drank.

Breaking with Conformity

To make a point, his booze was the ooze of his soul—it was his obscene gesture to the world in which he had grown up, the world in which his ancestors had settled in the Utah territory—the LDS church, which prohibited drinking.

He drank only as much as did his academic contemporaries of the time, which is to say, a fair bit. But he never missed a day.

He was rarely out of control. Science was his life, and he would not let anything stand in the way of his muse.

So in 1960, after a marriage of nearly 15 years' duration and three young daughters, my stepmother-to-be arrived on the scene.

She was this vivacious woman from Eastern Europe, a far cry from the sheltered world of Mormonism in which he'd grown up.

He was this maverick scientist, a far cry from the strictures of her established European priorities.

It was a match made in heaven. Their love affair, that is.

During the time they were dating, my father still lived at home. Each was swept off their feet by the other. They fell in love with the illusion they thought the other was.

The Family Breaks Up

During this time, my father left my mother. I was the eldest of the three girls; when I was born, my mother told my father she no longer wanted to be a scientist, but to stay home and raise babies.

He was shocked. This was the 1950s, mind you.

She was a lab technician, and would later become a nurse. She worked part time during my childhood. Yet, my father ached for a woman who would be a helpmeet.

He found that in my stepmother to be.

I enjoyed being around my father and stepmother; I could tell they were in love.

This, I did not begrudge him, as he was happy. I was distraught at my mother's unhappiness.

So, when my father announced what I expected—that he and my stepmother to be would marry, I was overjoyed. I looked forward to being an intact family again.

What I did not expect was that my stepmother was someone much more complex than I had seen.

My Stepmother Was a Controlling Woman

Within a month after the marriage, the fights started. She had her ideas, and she was headstrong. I don't remember the substance of the fights, just the tenor. She wanted her way—it was what she was accustomed to.

My father's world was rocked again, but in an entirely new way. He took to drinking to excess, for the first time. This was during the binges that would characterize his marriage to my stepmother.

He was crushed. The woman with the personality he admired and the body he loved was trying to cope with life as a green-card resident in the state of Utah, a place she called "the ends of the earth."

A psychologist friend of my father said the remarriage was a bad idea.

My stepmother barely spoke English, her son spoke even less. Four people lived in one house, none of whom could communicate effectively with more than one of the others.

Still, there was a lot of love. Clearly, they loved each other. Their love affair was one of the great passions of their time. The tumult they also lived was remarkable, too.

The fights were at night, not every night, not every week. But many nights, for eight years. But when they occurred, they were long and loud, with sobbing and howling coming from doors down the hall, into my room. My stepbrother interceded.

Too much alcohol and too many sleeping pills invaded their world, a world in which they were in way over their heads.

My parents were busy, no denying that. My father wanted my stepmother as his wife, first and foremost. The welfare of his daughters came second.

Looking After the Family

As the first-born, I was responsible for a lot of the cooking, shopping, laundry and a fair bit of the cleaning. We did have a woman once a week to clean the entire house; it was my job to clean specific rooms in the meantime.

I loved my father; I loved my stepmother. I loved being in a family again. But I did not love the stress that the dysfunction of this blended family played out for the eight years of the remarriage.

In marrying my father, my stepmother had to defect. She had to defect from then-Communist Poland, just to stay in the U.S.

It would be nearly a decade before she was allowed to return to Poland; it was nearly a decade before the Polish government allowed her own mother to visit.

In marrying my father, she had to divorce her own husband, a high-ranking economist with the Polish government.

This she did, by proxy. He created a scandal that echoed throughout Poland.

All this stress scarred my stepmother.

She found me difficult, willful.

I Was in the Way

In reality, I was at the wrong age for her to be my stepmother. I loved my father, and we were close. I looked up to him; largely, I ignored her.

She found my younger sisters more malleable. To be certain, they were. They were not 12 when my father remarried.

To look at this from my stepmother's perspective, I was in her way. My father's relationship with me stood in her way. It is not much more complex than that.

She was a loving woman, she was a selfish woman. She was kind, she was cruel. She was beautiful, she was an old woman with a mean soul.

She would give you everything, she would give you nothing.

She was a mass of contradictions. She is human. I loved her, I hated her.

I used to wonder when the world would end. I used to hope that it would.

When my father died, eight years after he remarried, that world did end.

My stepmother still teaches at the University. We do not speak.

Epilogue

My stepmother died on November 30, 2008. We had not spoken since 1996. I now look for ways to repair the scars—not only my scars, but the scars everyone endures in these situations—to look past human suffering in all things human: life, death, remarriage.

My Father's Mysterious New Life

Michelle Lupton

As a teenager, the author felt abandoned when her father moved to remote Pitcairn Island—but imagined him frequently as living a picturesque life at the side of his beautiful new wife. But when she visits him years later, she finds that island life is far from idyllic, and that her misgivings about her father have changed. She is able to forge a new bond with him.

As a child, I saw *Bounty*, the 1984 film starring Mel Gibson as Fletcher Christian. It is based on the true story of the mutiny on HMS *Bounty*, which set sail in 1787 to Tahiti to collect breadfruit plants and carry them to the West Indies to use as cheap fodder for slaves. Once the ship had left Tahiti Christian led a mutiny, rescued his men from the cruel grip of the tyrant Captain Bligh, and took his Tahitian princess to a paradise island where they could live in harmony and in hiding from the British authorities.

I was eight, and the film was a favourite because my father, who was divorced from my mother, was dating the real-life version of Christian's love in the movie. Her name was Brenda Christian. A direct descendant of Fletcher, she was brought up on Pitcairn Island, the remote hiding place of the mutineers whose descendants live there to this day. After marrying a British man, she had moved to the UK, separated from him—and then met my dad.

To me, she seemed every bit the Polynesian princess, mysterious and exotic with black hair to her waist. In summer she went without shoes; carvings, a map of the island and a real

Michelle Lupton, "First Person," *The Guardian*, April 9, 2007. Reproduced by permission of Guardian News Service, LTD.

grass skirt hung on the walls of her home. Most teenagers see their parents as boring, but Brenda was interesting and alluring.

My Stepmother Was Glamorous

My parents had divorced when I was six and my father, a retail manager for the army, was often on the move. My sisters and I saw him rarely: he wasn't really a father figure, more of a fun dad who took us out. And while we looked forward to his visits, we knew we couldn't rely on him as we relied on our mother.

I was 15 when he married Brenda in 1997. Suddenly he had a whole new stepfamily to look after, and by this stage we saw him only once a year. Then, when I was 17, the unthinkable happened: my stepsister wrote to me and mentioned that we probably knew my father and Brenda were moving to Pitcairn.

It was the first I had heard of any such plans, but when I confronted dad over the phone he denied any definite arrangements. It wasn't until Easter time, on a visit, that he told me and my sisters he was leaving for Pitcairn in a few weeks. He made it sound exciting and asked how we felt about him going.

Not wishing to ruin the last time we would be together (or cause a scene because we were in a restaurant), we said we didn't mind. But while he was the one going to a tiny island, it left my sisters and I feeling deserted.

Now he couldn't have been any less accessible. Pitcairn is no more than a tiny volcanic rock in the middle of the Pacific Ocean. Two miles in radius, and 300 miles from the nearest inhabited island, with no airport, it is one of the most remote places in the world.

There is no place for boats to dock, the only means of leaving and arriving is via specially built long boats that are expertly manoeuvred to meet ships that anchor away from the rocky shore. Only around 50 people are permanent residents.

It was a turning point in our relationship because, even though he had not been a great father before, I still held out hope that he would be. Now, it seemed, I would never have in him the father I had hoped for.

He never phoned—it was simply too expensive. There was no internet and only one satellite phone. A letter could take months to arrive depending on when a ship happened to call, and whether it was willing to take a sack of mail. When letters did arrive, they largely described day-to-day goings-on.

Dad never asked about us because he simply didn't know what was going on in our lives. But he was living the dream of an uncomplicated life, and this thought at least made the situation easier to bear.

My Father's Life Seemed Like a Dream

The movies and books that have been written about the story of Pitcairn Island have been criticised for offering a rose-tinted version of events. Captain Bligh may not have been any more of a cold-hearted tyrant than the average captain trying to control his men. Christian may have kidnapped the Tahitian men and women who went to Pitcairn. In a similar theme, my impression of the island, in first light a romantic one, became, on closer inspection, more sinister.

In stark contrast to the idyllic fantasy, I, along with the rest of the world, had my eyes opened to a dark secret when, in 2002, I heard the news that some of the islanders were to face trial for child molestation. Later I learned the full extent of these accusations. My step-uncle, Steve Christian, was being accused of six rapes and four indecent assaults. The other men on trial were his son Randy, father-in-law Len Brown, brother-in-law Dave Brown and his friends Dennis Christian and Terry Young. They were accused—and would later be found guilty—of systematic abuse of young girls spanning decades and generations. The island no longer seemed a haven where my father had escaped the rat race, but an iniquitous place where terrible things had been allowed to occur.

When, a few months later, I graduated from university, I was at a crossroads, and decided I wanted to visit Pitcairn. I knew my dad wasn't going to come back—so I decided to go to him.

Getting there was a real challenge. I had to take a tiny plane to the farthest of the Polynesian islands that runs only once a week. I then met with a tiny catamaran in Mangareva.

We set out just as it was getting dark, but during the night a storm erupted. There was very heavy rain and high wind. The swells were strong enough to knock you off your feet. Seasickness mixed with nerves about seeing my dad. A crossing that usually took two days took three. Because the weather was so severe we had to scramble from a dinghy on to the rocks on the far side of the island. My dad and stepmum clambered over to meet me. Brenda, born a Pitcairner, arrived first, my dad further behind, barefoot and tanned. He gave me a hug, then I held on for dear life while our quad bike raced over thick mud.

Far from Paradise

In many ways; Pitcairn looked perfect. The island is harsh and rugged but also green and peaceful. The islanders work together to man the long boats, their only means of connection to the passing ships. Days are spent fishing, growing food or making wood carvings to sell to the cruise ships that sometimes call. Everyone looks after one another's children; it was hard to work out who belonged to whom.

But I found my stepfamily in a fragmented state. My stepmum was the island police officer and, as such, was helping to bring her own brother, nephew and other relatives to trial. She was scarcely speaking to her brother at all, and her relatives would not open up to me—an outsider, and a British one at that. Many islanders were in a state of denial. Several women were openly defending their partners. But through this, my dad, Brenda and a few others bravely went against the common opinion and refused to defend the accused's alleged actions, preferring instead to allow a fair trial to decide.

It was not the reunion I had expected, but it was from this strange course of events that I formed a new-found respect for my father and stepmother. My dad, like me, was considered an outsider, and I think it helped him to have someone to confide in.

It also helped me to see him as a vulnerable person, not as the dad who abandoned my sisters and me, but as a man who would stand by his wife through thick and thin. I realised that as an adult I had to put aside the resentment I felt towards him for leaving, and just make the most of what we had.

I lived for four months on Pitcairn. I learned to fish with just a hook and line, snorkelled, and spent my days living the island way of life. It was the longest period of time I had spent in my dad's company since I was six. We went on long walks—and talks—around the island. My favourite place was "the highest point", a steep climb to a flat-topped hill from which you can see the whole island and the ocean beyond, a full 360 degrees. In the evenings we would play card games and sit and chat; it was at times like these that I really got to know my father again.

I left Pitcairn three years ago, but I hear from my dad much more now. Email has arrived in his life, and every couple of months he sends through news. I am happy that I can picture where he is and get on with my own life. I no longer have the romantic notion of Pitcairn as a perfect deserted island, and no longer have hopes for a perfect family.

But I think, in its place, I found something nearly as good; for while the dream didn't really exist, I found I didn't need it any more.

The Man I Call "Dad" Is the Man Who Raised Me

Marc Lynott

As a kid, the author idolizes his dad, and warms up slowly to his new stepdad. But as he grows older, he realizes that Jim, his stepdad, fulfills all his needs for a father figure, and that he cannnot relate to his irascible biological father anymore. Still, spending Father's Day with the man who raised him makes him feel as though he's betraying the man who brought him into the world. Marc Lynott is the pseudonym of a writer living in New York.

I hate Father's Day. Not because I have an abiding distaste for cologne, golf or books by Bill Cosby. The reason I hate Father's Day is because I have two dads, and come the third Sunday of every June, I feel like I'm letting them both down.

I didn't always feel this way. Father's Day and I actually got off to a good start. Even though my parents divorced when I was 4, they always accommodated each other so that my brother and I could spend Father's Day with our dad, whether the holiday fell on his designated weekend or not. Back then, when I was just a little pisher [a young squirt], Father's Day was a gas. I'd make my dad a card at school—usually having something to do with baseball—and then go with my mom to the mall to buy him a book or a CD. I'd always end up getting something, too. Then I'd go to my dad's house, where he'd always planned something special: a baseball game, a fishing trip, a drive to a wildlife reserve to watch birds and catch frogs. For sheer good times, Father's Day was just a notch or two below my own birthday.

Marc Lynott, "My Two Dads," Salon.com, 15 June 15, 2008. This article first appeared in Salon.com, at http://www.salon.com. An online version remains in the Salon archives. Reprinted with permission.

The first ripples started, unsurprisingly, when I got a new father. The first time I met Jim (names and identifying details have been changed), I was reading in my room when my mom called for me to come downstairs. There he was: a short guy with buggy eyes, a big belly and a bushy beard. He didn't have much in the way of books or games to offer, but something about him suggested ease, a marked contrast to my dad, who'd fly into a frightening rage at the drop of a Coke. I began to look forward to Jim's visits. When my Mom said they were getting married, I didn't mind.

Tensions Arise

Dad liked Jim less than I did. I quickly learned not to mention his name, which Dad drew out into three syllables whenever he said it, as if it was a schoolyard tease. Often, that tease would be incorporated into soliloquies about my mother's "fragile ego" or "selfish nature." Dad avoided encounters with Jim, dropping us off at the curb rather than walking us to the door of mom's house. Years later, I learned that early one morning, Dad showed up at Mom's house and knocked on the front door. When Jim answered, my dad poked his finger in his chest and told him he'd better not challenge his fatherhood, then turned around and left. My father needn't have worried. Jim was nowhere near as much of a threat to our relationship as he was.

Some men are meant to be fathers. But not necessarily fathers to children of any age. When my brother and I were still young enough to be bribed with a book or silenced with a yell, Dad was great. The problems began when the words "no" and "why" became a bigger part of our vocabularies. My dad's the kind of guy who spits four-syllable curse words at other drivers, sees insults where others see observations and prefers volume to reason. Jim's hero was Albert Einstein. He was more comfortable to be around. Gradually, he became the dad

I would go to for help with homework, to fix toys or to talk to teachers. He offered some solace.

The First Awkward Father's Day

My father was also looking for peace. For a time, he found it in religion, taking my brother and me to Temple when we'd never gone before. Then he put time and money into horses and fine-art dealing. That money didn't come back. Eventually, he found what he was looking for: a tall, slender, heavily made-up lady with a strange accent. The second time I met Olga was the day she moved in with him.

The first Father's Day with Olga was a bitch. Our cards and books paled beside her gift of a shiny new watch. Rather than go somewhere, we stayed at home and had an awkward dinner. In retrospect, you can't begrudge a middle-aged divorcé for falling in love. But 12-year-olds don't do romantic sympathy so well. I was mad that there was an interloper in the house. Jim had been introduced gradually, but that didn't happen with Olga. My brother and I had to share a bedroom when mine was converted into her office. Instead of bringing a baseball glove to the park, my dad now brought her. My father and Olga would have a private discussion, then return to tell my brother and me that we had to improve our manners or clean our rooms or lose weight. They got married. Our house became their house. Father's Days weren't much like birthdays anymore.

The Family Expands and Blends

Shortly before dad met Olga, my mother had a baby; Jim had become a father, and I, a stepbrother. We now had a legitimate reason to celebrate Father's Day with him, too, though not on the official day, which we still spent with our dad. And as for our dad, we gave Jim cards—usually humorous ones ("Far Side" was a favorite)—and gifts, now bought with our own money. It was a good day, but something gnawed at me. Something like betrayal.

As I got older, my relationship with my father continued to crumble. The things we'd once bonded over turned into breaking points. He lost interest in sports, fiction and, seemingly, anything we all might plausibly enjoy. He became enraptured with *Kabbalah* [the mystical aspect of Judaism] and *Rosicrucianism* [secret society of mystics] to which Olga had introduced him. Alternating weekends dwindled into occasional visits. We managed to fit plenty of fights into less time. The night before my bar mitzvah, he called to say he wouldn't be coming. Father's Days would come and go, with the only communication between us his angry phone calls the following Monday, during which he'd berate me for shitting on his fatherhood. It was hard not to agree.

It took a few years for me to call Jim "Dad," or, rather, "Daddy." I'd never used the word "stepfather" with Jim. It seemed so cold, so formal, like something you'd call a cartoon villain. I called him Jim. But when my sister was born, I made the switch. It took time to get used to. Even now, I find myself saying it softly in public. When people get confused about which man I'm referring to, I'll often use the terms "real" for my biological dad and "fake" for my stepdad. It started as a joke, but it stuck.

I guess I believe a father is a man who performs the duties a father should. Jim is my father. He has done everything I imagine a "real" dad is supposed to do. Yet, I can't quite shake the blues on Father's Day. I feel like the guilt over my "real" dad is unfair to Jim.

Maybe my dad is right and I'm a bad son. I was too eager to shift my affection to an easier relationship, too willing to loosen my ties with him over childhood slights. Maybe the fact that I'll be sending my dad a two-sentence e-mail this Father's Day, which is what I've done the last 10 years, means I'm a dick. But I made a choice, and his name was Jim. And come Father's Day, he's the one I'll hug, give a gift to, and say "I love you" to. And I'll feel like shit all day. Happy Father's Day? No, not really.

My Real Father Is Not My Dad

Sarah Ivens

Her biological father was an adulterer, and after her parents divorced when she was six, the author grew up without him. When her mother remarried, she developed a strong relationship with her stepdad. Becoming a successful professional, she realizes that she resents her real father's pride over her accomplishments, and that she no longer craves his attention. Sarah Ivens is a British journalist and the editor-in-chief of OK! Magazine.

My father is very proud of my achievements. On his desk at work is a mini-shrine to me. There are pictures and copies of my articles and when visitors ask what it's all about, he happily fills them in on his lovely daughter, who inherited his looks and good luck. All fathers are proud of their daughters, so this isn't weird. What is strange is that I haven't spoken to him for 18 years.

When I last saw him 10 years ago, he didn't recognise me. But now I'm a success, he's showing an interest. What a shame he didn't feel the same when I was an 11-year-old desperately in need of her father's affection.

Finding out about my errant father's pride unnerves me. I pushed him to the back of my mind when he pushed me aside. So when a long-lost family acquaintance (met by chance) revealed his renewed interest in me, I felt scared (that he'd try to find me), angry (that he was taking credit) and upset (should I contact him, shouldn't I?).

I'm not the only one. At a time when Kelly Holmes [English middle-distance runner] should be celebrating with close family and thanking them for backing her bid for Olympic

Sarah Ivens, "My Real Father Doesn't Matter Any More," *The Guardian*, guardian.co.uk, September 26, 2004. Reproduced by permission of Guardian News Service, LTD.

glory when it was just a distant dream, she is having to answer questions about the 'proud' father who claims she got her sporting ability from him. He disappeared when she was a toddler, yet now there's glamour, and possibly cash, involved, he wants a piece of the action. Derrick Holmes says he is 'hurt and upset' by her claims. 'Kelly assumes I'm only interested now she is so famous.'

Blood Is Not Thicker than Water

Of course she does! Why didn't he come forward when she was at school or a struggling athlete? How bizarre he comes forward only when Tom Cruise starts taking an interest [sic]. Which must be galling for Kelly and the man who raised her as his own, her only 'real father', her stepfather. There's an old-fashioned view that blood is thicker than water. Kelly and me are proof that this is not so. By 2010, there will be more stepfamilies than traditional ones in the UK and middle[-class] England and the Church of England think this is terrible. I think that, in this age of divorce, offering children stability is good. I'm lucky to have a stepfather who is as real to me as any father.

My parents divorced when I was six. My father was an adulterer who made my mother's life hell. I remember him being particularly gruesome to Mum one day and then taking me out and buying me a 'Daddy's Girl' T-shirt to wind her up. That day, I was the pawn in one of his many games. Eventually, my mother took the brave step of rescuing my one-year-old brother James and me from an unhappy home and setting up a smaller family unit.

Fighting Negative Perceptions

Single-parent families weren't so common in the early 1980s but she fought against the stereotypes, got a good job as a chef and picked me up from school every day. The neighbours gossiped and good friends suddenly disappeared as they feared my mother would be after their husbands, but, despite the inevitable distress, I look back on the five years that followed with fondness. My mother was tired and sometimes tearful, but life was easier without the arguments and lies. I recall all the clucking females in the family being worried that James would miss having a male influence around but I enjoyed our new girls' lifestyle.

Because I had the help of my grandmother and various aunts, in time I realised that not coming from a conventional family didn't matter, although I was envious of other girls my age and their conventional family lives. I was aware that Dad not living at home made me different, somehow less fortunate and freakish. My mother was careful not to poison us against our father and the lawyers granted him weekend access. Every Saturday, James and me would sit by the front door waiting for his arrival with great anticipation. He bought me a Care Bear every time he let me down; soon, I had the whole Care Bear collection.

Too often, after a few hours had passed, the phone would ring, he would cancel on us and my mother would be left to pick up the pieces. I remember one Saturday I was particularly excited because my father had promised me tickets to an important Spurs game at White Hart Lane. He gave my ticket to his current flame and my mother consoled me with a video—*Annie*. It's a film I still hate with a passion.

Broken Promises

On the few times he did turn up, the promised visits to the zoo or to a football match never materialised. Instead, we'd be taken to the homes of various new girlfriends and plonked in front of a television. I would be told to keep an eye on James while they disappeared to the bedroom. I felt crushed by his lack of interest. I was convinced I must be irritating, boring or ugly. After all, men are supposed to adore their daughters. But he showed no interest in me and my life. However simple my chatter may have seemed between the ages of seven and 10, my heart would break a little every time he ignored me.

Who knows how these early fears of my own self-worth have shaped my adult life? On paper, I'm not a failure, so perhaps his neglect pushed me to prove that I could be more than a discarded daughter: 'Hey, my dad doesn't want to know me but I might be able to persuade other people to love me.' Kelly Holmes behaved with incredible dignity when her biological father tried to muscle his way back into her life last month, but who knows what early childhood disappointment she went through? Maybe winning on the track became a way of compensating.

My mother, unsurprisingly, wasn't very interested in finding romance after her marriage ended. Between looking after us, running a home and working every day, she didn't have the time or the energy to pursue a relationship. Various men asked her out, and I remember one exciting Valentine's Day when 50 orchids were delivered to our house from an admirer. As an adult, I can understand she didn't want to introduce a stream of different men to her young children just to improve her self-confidence or social life.

A New Father

Then one day, when I was 10 and James was five, she sat us down and said that a man who came into the restaurant where she worked had asked her out and that she had accepted. This seemed fine to me, rather exciting, in fact, as men were rare visitors to our home. Date night soon arrived and I danced about the lounge trying to get his attention while James, who didn't appreciate the prospect of another man vying for his mother's affection, sulked and threw plastic dinosaurs at him.

I decided I liked him for childlike reasons: he had a black car like the one in *Knight Rider* and he, too, supported Tottenham Hotspur. What else could matter to a 10-year-old? In the weeks that followed, I realised romance was in the air because my mother started paying more attention to her appearance. She experimented with hairstyles and we started going swimming, her to tone up and me to learn how to dive.

Their dates became more frequent and, as my natural father's interest in me hit an all-time low—I would go without seeing him for six weeks at a time—Keith became a more positive influence in my life. He paid us the attention we craved and, most important, he did things to make my mum happier than I had ever seen her. The only time I can remember being upset was when I called him Uncle Keith and he told me not to. Growing up as I did, surrounded by aunts, I was just doing what I thought was polite. I didn't realise that a few days later he was going to propose to my mother and that he loved her so much he wanted to take her children as his own. He didn't want to be our uncle—he wanted to be our father.

Not a Charity Case

When my mother told me she was going to marry Keith, I took it as a compliment. In my 10-year-old head, I thought that, for him, getting a beautiful wife and two well-behaved children was a blessing. I didn't realise back then the stigma he had to take on and the unnecessary comments he received from those around him about us being a charity case.

They were married within a year, and I sat proudly in the front row of a London register office as a bridesmaid, with a beautiful bouquet and vintage velvet frock coat. I remember thinking after the reception: 'I'll have to look after myself now. Mum will be busy looking after her new husband', and I became more independent from that day on. The challenges I faced as a pre-teen have shaped my character to this day. I prefer doing things on my own to relying on anyone else and don't suffer fools gladly. I'm a sharp judge of character and can't even pretend to like people I assume are dishonest or unkind—like my real father.

Within a year, I had a new father, a new house, new school and a new surname—and a new brother, William. My mother fell pregnant three months after the wedding. She has since told me that she would have loved to have given James and me more time to settle into our new life but, at 37, she didn't have time to waste. I wish we'd had a little more time, too, and didn't understand why my life had been turned upside down quite so drastically.

Now that he had a natural child who would automatically receive anything should my mother or Keith die, he decided to look into legally adopting us. Hours and hours of meetings with social workers followed, which made me feel even more different from the new, fabulous friends I'd fought to make in my new town.

Being Abandoned Once Again

Deep down, I assumed the thought of having his children adopted would kick my real father into reality. He'd rebel and fight to keep us and the trips to the football game would resume. But a social worker told me quite harshly that once he'd established that signing his rights away would mean he wouldn't have any financial responsibilities to us, he practically begged her for the pen.

Despite referring to my stepfather as my father at school and taking his name, I couldn't bring myself to call him 'Dad' for three years. The night I finally did so was quite ordinary. I was watching *Top of the Pops* with my brothers, when he came in from work and handed us our usual Friday night goodie bag of sweets. I said: "Thanks, Dad" and carried on watching Bros. After years of trying to say that one small word, it felt very natural and much better than calling him Keith or not referring to him as anything in company. A few years later, my mother told me that he had returned to her in the kitchen, his eyes twinkling and a huge smile on his face.

I have seen my natural father once since. I was about 19 and shopping with a friend when I heard a voice I recognised. I knew it was him and turned round to see what his reaction would be. He carried on his conversation, looked me up and down and turned back again with no flicker of recognition. I felt a wave of nausea and stumbled away before bursting into tears. My friend followed me in horror and couldn't understand my mad ramblings. I'd been so embarrassed about my unconventional double life that I had told no one. Later, I felt relieved he didn't know me, that he had never been a major influence on my life.

Far from the stereotype of an unhappy stepfamily, I feel lucky we were given a second chance. In return for my thoughtless father, I got a kind, loyal and witty one. I have not seen my real father for 10 years and hope I never do. To find out about his office shrine to me is a shock. Keith paid my way through university, supported me when I was dumped by cruel boyfriends, walked me up the aisle on my wedding day and is incredibly proud of my career.

Yes, he has a picture of me on his desk and carries the latest article I've written in his briefcase. But he's allowed to. He's my dad.

Chapter 2

Parenting in Blended Families

Most Families Do Not Blend

Ron Deal, Interviewed by Duane Careb and Jim Mueller

In this interview, Ron Deal talks about the realities of everyday stepfamilies—especially the fact that most have a hard time growing together. He also speaks about the risks parents take when choosing a new partner, and the possible rejection by children of previous or new marriages. Ron Deal is a licensed marriage and family therapist, a certified family life educator, a certified family wellness instructor, and a member of the Stepfamily Association of America's Advisory Council. Duane Careb is a contributing author for Growthtrac, a Christian online marriage support Web site, founded by Jim Mueller and his wife.

Growthtrac: How prevalent are stepfamilies today in this generation?

Ron Deal: Currently in the United States, one out of three Americans has a step-relationship of some kind. Either they are a stepparent, a stepchild, a stepsibling; but they have a step-relationship of one sort or another. Approximately one half of us will have a step-relationship at some point in our life time, if the predictions hold true. So stepfamilies are very, very prevalent in our society.

I noticed in your book, the "Smart Stepfamily," that you refer to them as "stepfamilies," not "blended families." Is there a real difference there?

There is a real difference. To be honest, most stepfamilies don't blend. And the joke we like to tell is if they do blend, somebody gets creamed in the process. The idea is that there is a step-relationship, meaning there is something different about the relationship between at least two people in the home—they're not a blood relative to one another. So they're

Duane Careb and Jim Mueller, "A Conversation With Ron Deal," Growthtrac.com, February 7, 2005. Reproduced by permission.

a step removed from that. Blended families carry the idea that everybody in the family has blended, that all the relationships are equal or the same. And that really isn't the truth. It really becomes more of a fantasy.

You talk about this concept of "Crock Pot Stepfamilies." Can you explain that for us?

The idea is, how do you cook a stepfamily? If you were in the kitchen and you started to blend some ingredients, you might put them all in a bowl and start whipping them together until they combine thoroughly and completely. We've established that families just don't come together to that degree. But we have to employ some sort of style in order to bring the ingredients of this family together, and the blender doesn't work.

The microwave method is that we're gonna instantly fall in love with one another; we could just put it in for a few seconds and pop it out and everybody will be cooked and comfortable with each other. Some of the other approaches that I find stepfamilies using are things like the pressure cooker method, where pressuring messages are given to the children and to the adults of love and acceptance of one another. Again, sometimes that just doesn't happen and it certainly doesn't happen as quickly in the pressure cooker tins.

The crock pot method is the prescription that we want stepfamilies to utilize in trying to bring together the ingredients of their home—that is, their family members. This is the idea that you take the lid off the pot, you throw in all the ingredients, you put the lid on, turn it on low and you walk away. Two things happen, time and low heat combine in order to bring the ingredients together. Time refers to this idea that it takes the average stepfamily somewhere between five and seven years to really come together, to feel and function like a family.

Time Is a Decisive Factor

Low heat is the idea that the family is going to be intentional in allowing them to develop over time. That's what a crock pot does when it cooks ingredients. Families who have a crock pot mentality do a couple of things. First of all, they relax. And they understand that today we're not blended, we haven't combined and we're not done cooking; that we have lots of time to work on this and so today, we're going to accept where we are and we're gonna try to enjoy what we have and then we're gonna keep being intentional to move us ahead into the future. We're also not going to panic, because things haven't come together just quite yet. That's what a crock pot stepfamily looks like.

Ron, how important is it that siblings love and accept each other or love and accept the stepparent prior to the marriage?

I don't know that it's necessary. Again, the crock pot is gonna cook the different ingredients over time. It's helpful if the adults take the dating process slowly and give the children plenty of time to get used to the idea that they're going to be living in a stepfamily situation. When people rush into a remarriage they are ready for the remarriage, but their children generally are not and that brings with it more resistance from the children once the marriage has taken place.

Does that mean that the parents don't necessarily need to get "approval" from the stepchildren before getting married?

No, parents do not need their children's approval. However, the smart parent understands that leaving their children behind and entering a marriage that the children are not ready for simply is going to lead to stress and distress for the new stepfamily.

You mention that stepparents cannot afford to be insecure. What do you mean by that?

I mean they have to have tough skin. It's difficult to be a stepparent. One of the reasons for that is you're an outsider to the biological insiders who are related to one another and who love one another deeply. So the outsiders become the easy targets for stress and frustration.

Patience and Detachment

One of the things stepparents have to do is depersonalize the darts that are thrown at them. I call it "letting the bullet bounce." It's certainly gonna hurt when your stepson ignores you when you walk in the room. Instead of letting that bullet penetrate all the way to your heart where it can do a great amount of damage to your self-esteem and your sense of worth to the family, you have to let that bullet bounce at the skin. It will leave a bruise; it will perhaps leave a scar. But you're putting on some thick skin and reminding yourself that the comments are not necessarily about you.

They are more about the child's loss; they're about this transition in the home; they are about missing somebody else who's not in the home. And so you have to remember that you're valuable, and that God loves you, and that you have a worth that goes beyond getting the people in your home to fully accept you.

In regard to those bio-relationships, how critical is the unity factor to the success of the stepfamily?

A stepparent who is not fully supported by the biological parent really has no place in the family at all. They have no ability to discipline; they have no authority, because their authority is going to come from the biological parent. So the unity factor is critical to establishing the husband and the wife as the leaders of the home. They are the supreme command, if you will, and they cannot manage, direct, or be in charge of the home if they do not support one another. So a husband and wife need to negotiate the rules together, they need to make decisions together and they need to stick to their decisions and support each other in front of the kids. Sometimes making these changes as parents is the most difficult part of parenting. It requires some sacrifice on both the adults' part. But the unity is what will give the ability to lead the family.

Your research has produced some awesome [observations] about forgiveness in the stepfamily relationship itself. Can you elaborate on some of those?

In general, forgiveness is the thing that mends the hurts in our misguided attempts on love. In the end, it's really all we have to cover up our humanness. The fact is that we fail one another from time to time and so the forgiveness that God has granted us is the same thing that we are in turn to grant to one another. Specifically, I have found the forgiveness that needs to occur between ex-spouses is very critical to the success of a stepfamily home. They have to continue a relationship of shared parenting as the children move back and forth between homes. Too many times, ex-spouses end a marriage, move into a new marriage and still have not let go of the hurt and the pain from the previous relationship. It really sabotages the new stepfamily relationships.

What practical advice do you have for the stepparents who feel out of control and want to get back on track?

First and foremost, lower your expectations for the kind of relationship that you're developing with your stepchildren. I think stepparents expect too much of themselves. They want to have a good relationship with their stepchildren and that desire is very, very positive. However, if they work too hard at that and the children are not receiving of the stepparent's efforts, then its very easy to get discouraged and feel like you're failing.

But it really has more to do with whether or not the children are open to receiving you. So in lowering your expectations, we tell stepparents to remember the golden rule about developing a relationship with a stepchild and that is this: Let your stepchildren set the pace for their relationship with you. They need to be the ones who say when they're ready for affection. They need to be the ones who in effect let you know that your authority matters to them and that they welcome you being in charge of their life. It doesn't mean that you can't give some direction as a stepparent. In fact, I think one of the things stepparents can do when they discover that they've worked too hard is to simply step back, let the biological parent begin to step up to the plate and deal with the child a little bit more.

The Real Lives of Blended Families Do Not Follow TV Scripts

Jennifer Busse McClenon

TV is not a substitute for experience, the author finds out, when the wholesome pictures of The Brady Bunch *crumble under the reality of her own, new blended family. But once she has expelled notions of all-too-cozy harmony, she finds that she can still become a good stepmom. Jennifer Busse McClenon is a San Francisco Bay Area writer.*

Our front door bursts open and he yells, "Hullo?" as if entering an abandoned warehouse. It's not so much a greeting as it is an assessment of occupancy. My stepson clomps inside and kicks off his large black tennis shoes with a thud against the scuffed wall of the entryway. His keys land on the table with a metallic crash as he visualizes the expanse of empty-house opportunity sprawled out before him. Limitless freedom, if only no one would answer.

"Hi, Danny!" I don't know why I suddenly sound like a "Romper Room" host. I offer an engaging follow-up to his palpable disappointment that the house is, of course, not empty. "How's it goin'?" Or that it's simply occupied by me.

I am a new stepmother. I have learned some basic truths.

In the year 2000, it was estimated that there were more stepfamilies than any other kinds of families in the United States. Still reeling from the fact that I was plucked by an angel from the fiery hell of dating after 35, I felt emotionally invincible for whatever the ordeal was about blending families. If it's that popular, it can't be that bad.

Besides, people like me. My kid likes me. Bring it on.

Jennifer Busse McClenon, "Blended Families: The Brady Bunch Fraud," *San Francisco Chronicle*, April 14, 2002. Reproduced by permission of the author.

Stepparents Require Toughness

I'm not sure the exact moment the gravity of what I was signing up for began to sink in. Stepteens. It sounds like something [horror filmmaker] Wes Craven has in development. Or maybe even he has his limits for the macabre.

Cookbooks don't prepare you to stir; it's understood that you just stick the spoon in and start blending. Panicked by the veneer of unspoken tension, I sought resources. Those I found were chock full of upbeat strategies and anecdotal triumphs ending with person after person unable to believe "how close we've all become."

Useless advice warned against obvious pitfalls: premature bonding, inappropriate disciplining and corrosive spoiling. Luckily, I soon learned that there is actually very little to screw up with stepteenagers, since minimal damage can occur between the front door opening and their bedroom door slamming.

Because blending families is a modern anthropological issue, I partially blame the media for my naivete—specifically the missing episodes from *The Brady Bunch.* The closest my generation came to seeing any blended-family strife was when Mike and Carol Brady decided to settle an argument about who has the easier job by switching roles.

Mike helps Carol's daughters with their cooking project, and Carol bones up on baseball. The results are disastrous, and hilarity ensues. The fact is, hilarity rarely ensues in real life—and even less frequently when teenagers are involved.

I have developed these basic tips to help those who suddenly find themselves in love with a wonderful person who first procreated more than 15 years ago:

- Don't take it personally. It's not you. There is little likelihood of teenagers wanting to spend time forming a relationship with anyone older than 30.

- Unwanted: dead or alive. You could have been missing for days, and your stepteens will not be particularly glad to see you. Indifference may be upgraded to acknowledgment if you happen to have a case of Diet Coke strapped to your back or a 10-spot for gas.
- Unwanted because you're uninvited. Their parents' divorce, dating and marriage are not natural acts for children to witness. When you usher in the trifecta of discomfort, your unparalleled happiness is their childhood casualty. A chipper stranger with a child in tow was not on their wish list.
- Reset your barometer. Indifference is a teenager's God-given right. Lowering the bar on behavioral expectations will not only avoid the continual feeling that you're a fat tourist with a camera-festooned Hawaiian shirt invading their sanctuary, but it can also bring about spontaneous joys.

Lowering Expectations

For instance, "Uh, Jennifer? Do you know where the can opener is?" can actually seem like a touching dialogue signifying a building block of trust formed between you and the teen who tenderly chose to seek out your counsel in this trying time.

Protective armor. Try to get past the crusty exterior of baggy pants, melodic cell phones and listless shuffle to see the kid inside. While consumed by their own urgent plans, remember they're also grappling with stressful issues of modern young adulthood that you wouldn't trade with them for all the collagen in the world.

The bottom line when blending families with teenagers is that we're all just trying to figure out how this is supposed to work and not get in one another's way. No one has a script, a soundtrack, a cue or a clue.

You have a scant few years together, and someday they will regard you differently. Knowing it won't be anytime soon is the one thing you can count on. The American Psychological Association says that under the best conditions, it may take two to four years for a new stepfamily to adjust to living together. By then the teenagers will be college-bound.

Perhaps a slovenly psycho roommate from freshman dorm roulette will accelerate their appreciation of your role. Or not. But for now, keep your attitude positive, the refrigerator stocked and the barometer low.

And someday you just may not be able to believe how close you've become.

Bringing Together Parents and Stepparents

Lisa Cohn

After noticing how her children are pulled in different directions by traveling back and forth between parents, the author invites her ex-husband and her new husband's ex-wife to have dinner together. Despite an awkward start and odd silences, the families find a way to celebrate together, and include the many members of the blended families. Lisa Cohn and her husband, William Merkel, are the authors of One Family, Two Family, New Family: Stories and Advice for Stepfamilies. *Her work has also appeared in the* Christian Science Monitor, Mothering, Parenting, Mother Earth News, Brain, Child: The Magazine For Thinking Mothers *and* Your Stepfamily Magazine.

The last time I clashed with my ex-husband, Tripp, about how much time our son, Travis, would spend with each of us, Travis checked my face, then his dad's. He positioned himself halfway between us.

"Please," my son said, unfolding his small hands and extending them toward me and his dad. His blinked, as if fighting tears.

With my son's expression etched in my heart, I vowed that I would change. Somehow I needed to summon the superhuman strength to set aside my feelings of pain and distrust, to find a way to spend civil social time with both Travis and his dad. Then we wouldn't have to fight over him. And Travis wouldn't feel as if he had to completely separate his life with me—spent mostly at my house, in my neighborhood—from his life with his dad.

At that moment, I had an idea—but I knew it could lead to disaster.

Lisa Cohn, "Stepparents Sing Instead of Argue," *Christian Science Monitor*, September 17, 2003. Reproduced by permission of the author.

What if I invited my ex-husband, his wife, my new husband, his ex-wife, and our six children to a party?

Maybe—just maybe—we could create a new tradition that would give our kids the opportunity to feel connected to all their parents, at the same time, in the same place, if only for a few hours.

A Risky Proposal

First, I unveiled my idea to my husband, Bill, who responded by issuing one of his classic warnings. "The potential for disaster would never be more than 20 seconds away," he said.

I reminded him that just last Christmas, his daughter, Emily, had begged to invite her mother over to our house for Christmas.

Bill closed his eyes and scrunched up his face, as if gathering the courage to jump off a cliff.

"I think it's worth a try," he said. "But . . ."

When Bill and I presented my idea to Travis and my two stepchildren, we were greeted with silence.

Travis checked my eyes. Bill's kids, Emily and Chris, gazed at Bill's face. They seemed to be searching for the tight jaw line that signaled Bill's discomfort.

"If all our parents are at the same party, who's going to be in charge?" asked Chris.

"Since it's our party, Lisa and I will be in charge," said Bill.

"But my mom will make us all eat tofu," Travis said. "Then she'll make my dad run around to lose some weight, like she used to do when they were together."

"I'll serve food everyone likes," I promised. "Then I'll ask Bill to demonstrate his squat-jumper exercises, but I won't insist that your dad join in."

The kids laughed.

"Neat," said Travis. "Emily's and Chris's mom will meet my dad."

And so the preparations began.

An Idea Takes Shape

Bill spent what felt like months shopping for his ex-wife's favorite hors d'oeuvres.

"Linda likes homemade bread," he said, as we picked our way through the gourmet section of the grocery store.

"What's the matter with the stale white bread you feed the kids?" I asked.

He ignored me and immersed himself in memories of party planning with his ex.

"We used to have dinner parties, and we always bought Gouda cheese," he said.

Next he insisted on fresh shrimp.

"What's the matter with the sticky frozen stuff we usually eat?" I asked.

"Lisa, I'm not trying to woo Linda," Bill said, turning away from the food for the first time. "This is all about the kids. I want Linda to feel welcome and at home. If she feels comfortable, the kids will feel comfortable, and our party might actually be a success."

When our guests arrived for our party, we all shuffled around the dining-room table, mostly silent. My head pounded as I arranged the gourmet cheeses. I tried to think of something to say to Bill's ex-wife.

As we all gaped at the food, I counted the sweat droplets that appeared, one by one, on Bill's forehead.

A Stressful, Awkward Dinner

My stepchildren positioned themselves equidistant from Bill and his ex-wife and held that distance. If Bill moved to the right, Emily and Chris adjusted their stations; if their mother veered toward the kitchen, Emily and Chris followed her just so far.

Travis eschewed the equidistant rule in favor of gluing himself to the parent he had seen the least in recent days, in this case, his dad.

As the children danced around their parents, I worried about the possibility of calamity. I tried to think of something scintillating, opened my mouth, closed it, blushed.

Bill's eyebrows twitched, a sign that he thought his worst nightmares were about to come true.

I decided I couldn't bear the discomfort, worry, fear, and potential for embarrassment for one more minute. I silently prepared myself to send everyone home and proclaim the event a failure.

That's when 11-year-old Emily, 5-year-old Chris and 10-year-old Travis stepped forward.

"Hey, Dad," said Travis, leading his father to our living room. "Check out our new couch. It's supposed to look good with those scary masks that Bill nailed on the living room wall." Travis sat on our couch and patted the seat beside him.

"How about you sit right here, Mom?" asked Emily, choosing a spot on the couch a few feet from Travis. "How do you like where we put the TV?" She pointed to a television set wedged into a corner of the room. "It's way over there because we're not supposed to watch it."

Chris jogged into the kitchen and returned with a tray of shrimp and cheese. He passed it from guest to guest.

Breaking the Spell

The kids' efforts freed me to suggest we all sing "If You're Happy and You Know It, Clap Your Hands" for our baby, 8-month-old Allison.

Bill's wife launched immediately into the song, and Allison swung her legs.

"OK, how about 'Bingo'" said Linda, when we finished.

"There was a farmer, had a dog, and Bingo was his name-o . . ."

Everyone joined in.

Then Travis led us in a rendition of "Jingle Bells, Batman Smells, Robin Laid an Egg."

Even Bill joined in, belting out the song in a bass voice that once garnered him a position in a high school rock 'n' roll band.

Tripp smiled. The kids sang louder. Linda laughed.

For just a moment, the sounds that issued from our living room suggested a moment of joy, among family members. For just a moment, my wish for our children came true.

At that moment, we launched a tradition that has continued for five years—in spite of the potential for disaster.

A Different Kind of Mother's Day

Dawn Miller

Stepmothers are often left out of Mother's Day celebrations. After years of feeling awkward and unappreciated, the writer receives a card from her stepdaughter and finds that stepmotherhood is motherhood after all. Dawn Miller writes a column on life in blended families at TheStepfamilyLife.com.

Mother's Day is admittedly an awkward day for stepmoms. I'm not a mother—yet—just a stepmom to three. I was relieved to see our new church does not ask mothers to raise their hands and be recognized with a flower. I always felt non–flower-worthy at our old church—like I didn't qualify since there was no stepmom or "like a mom" category. Thankfully, our new church puts all the flowers in a box to the side and says if you'd like to honor someone for Mother's Day, pick a flower and give it to them—a pragmatic solution given the blended family nature of our times.

Even though I'm not a "real" mother—I engage in "mothering" behavior—I fret over the middle child's future and lack of direction after graduation, buy the books used by the oldest at college, bake them all cookies, ask them to keep their shoes off the furniture, and take the youngest shopping. I bought medicine when they were sick, learned how to cook so I could feed them, and played chauffeur until they learned to drive. I love my stepchildren—they are part of my family—and I feel an obligation to care for, nurture and encourage them. I'm still not a mother—and I know that—but I am much more than a friend.

Dawn Miller, "Mother's Day for Stepmoms," TheStepfamilyLife.com, May 14, 2006. Reproduced by permission of the author.

An Awkward Holiday

Yet Mother's Day remains problematic on many fronts for stepfamilies—and for us. My husband is grateful—and so am I—that his children have a mother who loves them—and I wouldn't want to rain on her special day in any way. So I don't like to make a big deal about Mother's Day—I expect to be second fiddle at best.

One of my stepmom friends would be fussed over by her stepchildren—because their real mother didn't want to be with her children on Mother's Day. The stepmom felt awkward about it and like she was in a place she shouldn't be. But these children had no other female authority figure to honor that day—so she was their princess paramount—the stepmom who doesn't mind a little gratitude, but isn't comfortable wearing the tiara of motherhood.

Unfortunately there's few options other than creativity—for acknowledging stepmoms for their "mom-like" behavior. The few cards for stepmothers out there are often trite, in short supply, and poorly or stodgily written. The term "stepmother" carries so many negative connotations that often the "like a mother" or more generic non-mother Mother's Day cards are at least marginally better than the stepmom cards. It is easier to find a Mother's Day card for an aunt who is "like a mother," than for a bona-fide stepmom. It's actually worse than trying to find a birthday card addressed to a stepparent—ick—Hallmark and the other greeting card companies are truly missing a market.

Against the Norm

What's sad is that people make even our stepchildren who want to do nice things for their stepmoms to acknowledge them—feel like they are going outside the norm. One of my stepmom friends relayed to me that her stepdaughter's elementary school class made planters as gifts for Mother's Day. When her stepdaughter asked for a plant so she could make a gift for her stepmom—whom she lives with half the time—the teacher balked. Eventually she let her make a second planter. If the little girl wanted to give her stepmom a gift to show she appreciates her support and care—why shouldn't she? Why does it have to be a big deal when the teacher had extra plants anyway?

Admittedly, my experience with the holiday has been spotty. To honor my first Mother's Day as a stepmom, the kids gave me a necklace and said nice things. The next year they didn't notice me at all—and I was crushed. Last year I concocted a scheme to leave town to visit my mother for the holiday, but cancelled my trip when my mother-in-law passed away a few days before Mother's Day. Instead my mother came to help us through our grief. As we sat in the car waiting for the funeral procession to start—the youngest one handed me a card from all three kids carrying a beautiful sentiment for Mother's Day.

With this kind of track record, I know the only thing to expect on Mother's Day is the unexpected. Then this morning my stepdaughter handed me a card—the most wonderful card—in which she wrote a long note about how much she appreciates me in her life and how she knows I love her. It was completely unexpected and exactly what I needed to hear—that the day in and day out struggle of raising a family are worth it, that the things we do 365 days a year are appreciated and noticed. It didn't matter that I wouldn't be toasted as the creme de la creme—just that the sentiment was said. And as I went through my day I pulled out that card and read it again and again.

It was the best Mother's Day I've ever had—for someone who's not a mother.

Stepfamilies Are Normal Families

Laurie McGough Hanson

The author, having experienced life in a stepfamily firsthand, imagines that becoming a stepmother should be easy for her. Yet when she marries a divorced man with children from his first marriage, she finds out that nothing comes easy in a blended family. Still, after many initial problems, the new family pulls together, one baby step at a time. Laurie McGough Hanson is the Pittsburgh Post-Gazette *editorial products and promotions coordinator.*

When my brother Matthew died recently, and I faced the traditional two-day viewing, my heart sank. I didn't want to talk to anyone. When James drove up from Columbia, Md., offering carte blanche assistance, I had just the job for him.

"Just circulate, talk to people, especially anyone who looks lost." James and I have had our ups and downs over the years, but I'll say this about him—he can talk to anybody about anything. Anywhere.

When he arrived at the funeral home, a huge weight lifted from my shoulders. Both days, he was there with me and more importantly, *for* me. James isn't my brother, cousin, uncle or in-law. But he's part of my family all the same. James Hanson is my 37-year-old stepson.

Becoming a Stepmother

When I married a divorced man with two children 16 years ago, I'd already been a stepdaughter and stepsister for years. I figured that would prepare me to become a stepmother. I figured wrong.

Laurie McGough Hanson, "Saturday Diary: True Confessions of a Stepmom," *Pittsburgh Post-Gazette*, April 19, 2003. http://www.post-gazette.com/forum/comm/20030419diary0419p2.asp.

When I first met Dave's kids, my fear of rejection was immediately replaced with confusion—these were really *tall* children.

Hey, wait a minute, they weren't even children, they were almost *adults*. James was 6 feet 3 inches and his 16-year-old sister already stood at 5 feet 9. Me? I'm barely 5 feet 3. And, not only was I too short to be their step-mom, I was way too *young*. Dave is 15 years older than I am. James and Carol were born three years apart when he was in his early twenties. Do the math. Yep, I'm closer in age to them than I am to their Dad.

Stepmothers have gotten a bad rap for years. We all know what Cinderella and Snow White had to put up with. But evil stepmothers at least had some direction. I was just a *clueless* stepmother.

We were a "poster stepfamily" at our wedding. Carol and James both stood up for their father as "Best Children." James gave an eloquent toast to the newlyweds, who then tripped off to Europe for a dream honeymoon. But a funny thing happened on the way back to the States—the kids were still there. And still a really big part of Dad's life. Duh, how'd I miss that?

Blending a Family

I think the biggest misconception about successfully "blending" a family is that it can be achieved on a schedule. Do this, expect that, demand this and everyone will adjust. But families don't grow on schedules and no book (trust me, there are hundreds available on Amazon.com) about the routes to successful stepparenting could have prepared me for the roller coaster role for which I'd signed on.

I'd married a man who had a whole family, a whole *life*, before I even met him. I was the outsider. An insecure outsider.

I was hurt that Dave's first concern when we were expecting a baby of our own was for his children's reaction. They didn't disappoint. I think the words "Yuck!" and "Gross!" were uttered a few times. And when Dave announced that he was taking his 17-year-old daughter skydiving, I paled.

"I took James so I have to take Carol," he argued. Excuse me? Throwing yourself out of a plane voluntarily is not something I'm going to let you do with a child of mine.

Ooops. Forgot. Not my child, I don't get a vote. In the midst of these seemingly endless mini-dramas, we forged our life together and welcomed two sons of our own.

Disaster Strikes

And just when I thought that I had the hang of the stepmother thing, the ultimate curve ball hit us all between the eyes. James was diagnosed with a rare form of cancer. Looking back, I'm ashamed to admit that I was as worried about my marriage as I was about my stepson's health.

For months, Dave drove James back and forth to chemotherapy. Then, each night, my husband sat on the porch swing and rocked for hours. Alone. I couldn't reach him, I couldn't share his pain. Because, no matter how my heart ached for his son, this is a child we did not share.

Well, miracles do happen and James has been cancer-free for eight years. But it was during that stressful time that the magic moment I think we all strive for in stepfamilies happened to James and me—my husband ceased being the only connection that we shared. James and I became real people to each other as I watched him drag first to Pitt, then Carnegie Mellon when he could barely sit up from the cancer and its treatment.

To this day, there are few people that I admire more than my stepson. We aren't super close, but we're family. Time does that to stepfamilies. It helps us create memories and histories—good and bad—of our own.

Two years ago, Dave, our sons and I attended my step-daughter's wedding in Michigan. She was beyond beautiful as she walked down the aisle with both her dad *and* mom, Dave's ex-wife Barb. Our boys and I sat in the front row next to Barb's husband, Ken. The night before, my own little four-some was graciously welcomed into Barb and Ken's home as guests. And, I had a great time.

Forging New Bonds

Who wudda ever thunk it could happen? Scenes like this are happening more and more today. Numbers don't lie: one out of every two marriages ends in divorce; 75 percent of all divorced people will eventually remarry; about 65 percent of remarriages involve children from a prior marriage, and one out of 3 Americans is now a stepparent, stepchild or stepsibling.

So, how did our blended family get to this picture-perfect point?

We all just sort of stumbled through it over the years. I credit my stepchildren for growing with me, never giving up on me and never calling me short, at least to my face. And I thank their dad for teaching me that a parent's unconditional love doesn't diminish just because the child grows up. What book could teach that?

What advice would I give a new stepmom? Sure, read a book about stepfamilies but don't be surprised if it doesn't give you the answers you want. Don't expect to like your step-children right away, but don't be surprised if you do. Don't think for a minute that your husband will stop being a father just because he's a new husband. Expect to make mistakes, lots of them.

And, don't be shocked if one day you find yourself thinking on your own about your stepchildren and how they're doing, being glad that they're well and happy. Because when I look at James and Carol today, I see two really neat, bright, interesting adults.

And, guess what? I had little to do with them growing up that way. Families come in all shapes and sizes. And the "step" in my stepfamily that used to be a canyon is now just a baby step. Forget the label. We're just a family.

Chapter 3

Toward a New Understanding of Family

Leaving Behind Traditional Views of Belonging

Natasha Sky

Many schoolbooks, the author finds, are lagging behind the times. While it becomes more and more common for children to grow up in blended and mixed-race families, families with a single mom, two moms, or two dads, schoolbooks still cling to traditional values, leading to confusion and frustration with modern kids and parents. New texts, she demands, should reflect new realities, and teach children that they belong, no matter what their families look like. Natasha Sky is a writer, artist, and activist. She created MultiracialSky.com, a Web site of resources for multiracial families.

My son was writing in his workbook the other day. We're homeschooling in the eclectic-semi-unschooling-style; the workbooks have been around for over a year—my kids think they're *fun*. The books are actually a great distraction for a cranky kid who is not going on the errand with Dad. This workbook came home with Rico from a trip to grandma's house. It's a general preschool-skills book. I've been happy with it so far (multiple races of kids; both genders) my only complaints are the coloring-in busywork (which he generally skips) and the staying to stereotyped gender roles—even for the anthropomorphised [humanlike] animal characters.

Rico is starting to read, but he doesn't sound out multiple unknown words on his own. So he asks me to read the directions at the top of each page. He turned the page, called me over, and I saw this picture:

The directions said, *Which puppies belong to this mama? Draw a line from the mother to her puppies.* I paused. I had to think of alternate directions. "What does it say?" Rico asked.

Natasha Sky, "Who Belongs?" AntiRacistParent.com, October 26, 2007. Reproduced by permission.

"Uh, it says, '*Which of these puppies looks like their daddy? Draw a line from the Daddy dog to the puppies that look like him.*'"

Mixing and Matching

I get it. It's a 'sorting' skill. But the matching and the 'which one doesn't belong' games bother me; it's all a matter of perspective. In their workbooks, my kids cross off items that would be graded 'wrong' in school. They X art supplies and sporting equipment off the toy shelf, and leave the cowboy hat and the violin—because at our house the basketball lives in the shed, the paints are in a downstairs cupboard, and the dress-up clothes and musical instruments are with the other inside toys. My kids find connections between all sorts of random pairs—a dog goes with a piano because they both can make a really loud noise. Okay. I value the creative thinking over the 'matching skill'.

After the workbook incident, I found myself singing this old Sesame Street song:

Three of these things belong together.

Three of these things are kind of the same.

Can you guess which one of these doesn't belong here?

Now it's time to play our game; it's time to play our game.

I know a mom (who has two White bio kids and one adopted child of color) who was posing for a photo with her husband and children at a large family gathering. This mom's brother—her children's uncle—started singing, "One of these things is not like the other . . ."

Society, school, and parents are passing down to the next generation arbitrary rules about what 'goes' together. Apple + Orange + Banana = FRUIT. Mother + Father + Baby = FAMILY. Today, the *baseline assumptions* about what a family looks like are the same as they were fifty years ago in the U.S. At best, elementary school curriculum offers a unit on, or at least a nod to, 'different' kinds of families. That 'traditional' family—1 mother, 1 father, and 2 or 3 children, all the same race—plagues all of us who fall outside that model.

Families of Today Are Diverse

There are a *lot* of us post-traditional families nowadays. We are multiracial families, single parent families, two-mom or two-dad families. We are foster families, 'chosen' families, blended families, and families with 4, 5, 7, or 10 children. We are families headed by grandparents, aunts, uncles, older sisters or brothers. Each one of us, a unit of two or more people caring for each other, each is a family. We are connected through love, blood, promises, circumstances, court decrees, and the daily grind. We are all kin.

As parents, we must be careful how we teach our kids about the concept of 'normal', and what we model for them about the weight and meaning of this subtle and powerful word. I want my kids to know that what they *are*, and their family composition, is normal—because it *is*. They do not have to (nor should they) change any part of themselves to feel they belong.

Belong where? Belong to what? First and most importantly, I want my children to belong to themselves, to be comfortable in their own mind and skin with who they are. I also want them to feel they belong to our immediate family, our extended families, their birth families and ancestors, their local community, their ethnic communities, and the world.

New Families Are 'Natural'

We are walking fine lines. I want to model valuing diversity in people and families, without implying one must be different from the majority to be significant. I want my children to be able to blend in (physically and socially) *if they choose to*, but never to suffer from personal, familial, or societal pressure to conform. I know we cannot escape some of these pressures; I want my children to be strong and proud and even defiant in the face of the pressure to 'match'.

We are raising independent souls here, free thinkers who will decide for themselves who and what belongs, or whether the rules are bogus and everyone should decide for themselves. Who belongs? It's up to them.

Growing Up in a Group Marriage

Laird Harrison

When he is nine, the writer's parents move in together with another married couple and their children. For several years, he experiences social stigma, awkward situations due to a lack of privacy, but also an unusual sense of camaraderie and generosity. When the families break up, Harrison mourns the loss of the bonds forged, and even though he does not replicate his parents' experiment, he has come to understand what made them try. Laird Harrison is a writer living in the San Francisco Bay Area. He has recently completed work on Children of a Future Age, *a novel about a group marriage in the 1970s and the children growing up in it.*

One day in the summer of 1971, my parents held hands, closed their eyes and jumped out of their conventional marriage into something strange and new. I was 9 years old at the time, and we were camping at Betsy Lake in the High Uintas Wilderness with another family of five. We were halfway into the camping trip when the six of us kids realized our parents had mixed and matched: My father was in the tent with their mother, and their father was in the tent with my mother.

No sound came from either tent. I remember the smell of mosquito repellent. I remember gray ripples in the lake, squirrels scrambling up pine bark and us kids nervously discussing. I remember trying to believe my life hadn't shot off its safe, predictable tracks.

Laird Harrison, "Scenes from a Group Marriage," Salon.com, June 4, 2008. This article first appeared in Salon.com, at http://www.salon.com. An online version remains in the Salon archives. Reprinted with permission.

Off the Beaten Path

Of course, it had. We began seeing the other family at least once a week; one of my parents spent each Sunday at their house and one of theirs at mine. And then we all moved in together. The arrangement felt uncomfortable, if only because no one else's parents were doing anything like it. One day, as I lay reading on my bed, the girls from the other family came downstairs with moving boxes in their arms. That night, the adults erected a screen to separate the dining room from the living room. In place of our dark varnished table and the buffet with its china and silver appeared a king-size bed. Downstairs, the salt-and-pepper sofa and the desk where my father tracked investments gave way to bunk beds for two of the girls. Over the next few days, my brother and I learned to grab for our bathrobes when our new sisters slipped through our room on the way to the toilet in the morning. They learned to duck behind closet doors when we trespassed through their bedroom on our way upstairs.

Fiction about the 1970s—including *The Ice Storm* or the new *Swingtown* TV series—typically depicts such experiments as frivolous and irresponsible. "How could they have done this to you?" my wife still asks me. It's true that boredom was an element in my parents' motivation. It's also true that the arrangement embarrassed me in front of my friends, and that it threw me off balance at a nervous time of life. But behind that—at least sometimes—lay an idealism that has disappeared from the public recollection.

My parents saw themselves as part of a movement, promulgated in visionary writings like Alvin Toffler's "Future Shock." The notion was that an adult could simultaneously maintain more than one intimate relationship as long as all the partners agreed. The movement, which now calls itself "polyamory," is still going, though mostly underground. Webster's accepted the word two years ago [in 2006].

A Special Bond

But my parents didn't take a public stance. They kept their sex lives to themselves; they never suggested I should want to follow their example. And the communal household enjoyed a kind of camaraderie I have never felt since. I liked the party we made when all of us kids sat down to watch *Hogan's Heroes* or danced to the soundtrack from *Cabaret*. Over the next two years, I swapped books with my stepsisters, listened in awe to their stories of crushes, exchanged tips on teachers. Their father imparted his love of great music and their mother her passion for cooking. A sort of bond formed among the 10 of us.

I found out it was ending one day, after a tennis lesson, when my mother picked up my brother and me in her blue Dodge Dart with its painted butterflies. I knew from her silence something was wrong. She pulled into the parking lot of a drug store and sat for a moment. Without turning to face us, she said that the two families were splitting into separate households—but not in the original configurations. My father would live with the other woman, my mother with the other man.

I didn't ask for the story of the foursome's disintegration. Despite the intimacy of our crowded household, or perhaps because of it, we kids refrained from probing the details of the adults' love lives. Instead I stared at the smudged upholstery of the seat in front of me, feeling in my stomach as though we had just driven off a cliff.

Over the next few years, that falling sensation accelerated. My father married the other woman. The other man found a new lover and left my mother. I switched back and forth every six months between my parents' households. For the first time in my life, my mother let me see her tears. I learned to hide mine in my pillow.

Missing the Solace of Extended Families

Divorce is commonplace now, but group marriage is still weird, almost incomprehensible to most people. Only recently have I overcome the shame that used to make me gloss over that period when I told new friends the story of my life. But now, when I think back, I can see it wasn't the group marriage that cast a lasting shadow on my childhood; it was the divorce. For a few years I'd had something more than a family, then suddenly I had something less. And the loss was wrenching.

This year, my youngest son is 10, as I was at the beginning of my parents' odyssey. His brother is 14—close to my age at the end. I've felt for myself the stress that our hyper-individualist culture puts on families. Few of us live with extended family; fewer and fewer of us know our neighbors, go to church or belong to a social club. We measure success by the size of our houses and our paychecks. We see child rearing as a lifestyle choice, not a community endeavor. But two grown-ups sometimes aren't enough to pay the bills, to wipe the noses, to coach the soccer team and listen to the stories of schoolyard bullying. After 17 years, my wife and I are still passionate about each other. I have no desire to engage in the bold sort of experiment my parents took on. But sometimes, even when all four of us are home together, our world feels too small, and I understand the hope with which my parents blindly plunged into uncharted love.

Divorce Does Not Have to Be the End of Family

Constance Ahrons

Divorce is often seen as a major cause of resentment, fear, and confusion, for children and their parents. Yet while attending the wedding of her "ex-husband's daughter by his second wife," the author observes that divorce and remarriage can lead to new alliances, new families, and a broader and maybe better understanding of what it means to belong. Constance Ahrons is the author of The Good Divorce *and coauthor of* Divorced Families.

It was a sunny, unseasonably warm Sunday morning in October. In a quaint country inn in New Jersey, surrounded by a glorious autumn garden, my young grandchildren and I waited patiently for their Aunt Jennifer's wedding to begin. The white carpet was unrolled, the guests were assembled, and the harpist was playing Pachelbel's *Canon*.

A hush came over the guests. The first member of the bridal party appeared. Poised at the entry, she took a deep breath as she began her slow-paced walk down the white wedding path. Pauline, my grandchildren's stepgreat-grandmother, made her way down the aisle, pausing occasionally to greet family and friends. A round of applause spontaneously erupted. She had traveled fifteen hundred miles to be at her granddaughter's wedding, when only days before, a threatening illness made her presence doubtful.

Next in the grand parade came the best man, one of the groom's three brothers. Proudly, he made his way down the aisle and took his position, ready to be at his brother's side.

Constance Ahrons, *We're Still Family: What Grown Children Have to Say About Their Parents' Divorce*, New York: HarperCollins, 2004.

Then the two maids of honor, looking lovely in their flowing black chiffon gowns, made their appearance. My grandchildren started to wiggle and whisper: "It's Aunt Amy [my younger daughter]! And Christine [the longtime girlfriend who cohabits with Uncle Craig, my daughters' half-brother]!" As they walked down the aisle and moved slowly past us, special smiles were exchanged with my grandchildren—their nieces and nephew.

One Big Family

Seconds later, my youngest granddaughter pointed excitedly, exclaiming, "Here comes Mommy!" They waved excitedly as the next member of the bridal party, the matron of honor—*their mother, my daughter*—made her way down the path. She paused briefly at our row to exchange a fleeting greeting with her children.

Next, the groom, soon officially to be their "Uncle Andrew," with his mother's arm linked on his left, and his father on his right. The happy threesome joined the processional. Divorced from each other when Andrew was a child, his parents beamed in anticipation of the marriage of their eldest son.

Silence. All heads now turned to catch their first glimpse of the bride. Greeted with oohs and aahs, Aunt Jennifer was radiant as she walked arm in arm with her proud and elegant mother, their stepgrandmother, Grandma Susan. Sadly missed at that moment was the father of the bride, my former husband, who had passed away a few years earlier.

Complex Family Ties

When I told friends in California I was flying to the East Coast for a family wedding, I stumbled over how to explain my relationship to the bride. To some I explained: "She's my ex-husband's daughter by his second wife." To others, perhaps to be provocative and draw attention to the lack of kinship terms, I said, "She's my daughters' sister." Of course, technically she's my daughters' half-sister, but many years ago my daughters told me firmly that that term "half-sister" was utterly ridiculous. Jennifer wasn't a half anything, she was their *real* sister. Some of my friends thought it strange that I would be invited; others thought it even stranger that I would travel cross-country to attend.

The wedding reception brought an awkward moment or two, when some of the groom's guests asked a common question, "How was I related to the bride?" With some guilt at violating my daughters' dictum, but not knowing how else to identify our kinship, I answered, "She is my daughters' half-sister." A puzzled look. It was not that they didn't understand the relationship, but it seemed strange to them that I was a wedding guest. As we talked, a few guests noted how nice it was that I was there, and then with great elaboration told me stories about their own complex families. Some told me sad stories of families torn apart by divorce and remarriage, and others related happy stories of how their complex families of divorce had come together at family celebrations.

New Opportunities

At several points during this celebratory day, I happened to be standing next to the bride's mother when someone from the groom's side asked us how we were related. She or I pleasantly answered, "We used to be married to the same man." This response turned out to be a showstopper. The question asker was at a loss to respond. First and second wives aren't supposed to be amicable or even respectful toward one another. And certainly, first wives are not supposed to be included in their ex-husband's new families. And last of all, first and second wives shouldn't be willing to comfortably share the information of having a husband in common.

Although it may appear strange, my ex-husband's untimely death brought his second and first families closer together. I had mourned at his funeral and spent time with his family and friends for several days afterward. A different level of kinship formed, as we—his first and second families—shared our loss and sadness. Since then, we have chosen to join together at several family celebrations, which has added a deeper dimension to our feelings of family.

You may be thinking, "This is all so rational. There's no way my family could pull this off." Or perhaps, like the many people who have shared their stories with me over the years, you are nodding your head knowingly, remembering similar occasions in your own family. The truth is we are like many extended families rearranged by divorce. My ties to my ex-husband's family are not close but we care about one another. We seldom have contact outside of family occasions, but we know we're family. We hear stories of each other's comings and goings, transmitted to us through our mutual ties to my daughters, and now, through grandchildren. But if many families, like my own, continue to have relationships years after divorce, why don't we hear more about them?

Overcoming Old Stereotypes

Quite simply, it's because this is not the way it's supposed to be. My family, and the many others like mine, don't fit the ideal images we have about families. They appear strange because they're not tidy. There are "extra" people and relationships that don't exist in nuclear families and are awkward to describe because we don't have familiar and socially defined kinship terms to do so. Although families rearranged and expanded by divorce are rapidly growing and increasingly common, our resistance to accepting them as normal makes them appear deviant.

Societal change is painfully slow, which results in the situation wherein the current realities of family life come into conflict with our valued images. Sociologists call this difference "cultural lag," the difference between what is real and what we hold as ideal. This lag occurs because of our powerful resistance to acknowledging changes that challenge our basic beliefs about what's good and what's bad in our society.

Blending Families and Faiths

Barbara Miksch

While divorce and remarriage are often seen as dividers and possible threats to family life in general, the author shares her positive experience of not only living in a blended family by getting remarried, but also of bringing together two different faiths for all family members to share and partake in. Barbara Miksch tutors students in her Kansas home.

Being part of an interfaith marriage was not a new experience when I remarried. My first marriage was to a man who had been raised Presbyterian. Our son Michael was raised Jewish, but we also celebrated Christian holidays with my spouse's family.

My current spouse, Jim, is a very spiritual man who has enriched my experience when we worship together, whether in the synagogue or in his church. He is a member of a mainstream Presbyterian church where many of my close friends, as well as many of my son's close friends, belong. In fact, we met in a nonsectarian class, "Newly Single," sponsored by the Singles Ministry of his church. Jim, of course, loved introducing me to his friends as his "church lady," and then watching their response when he told them I was Jewish.

Interestingly, when Jim and I began dating, his son, Matthew, was engaged to a Jewish girl (they were both students in college at the time). His engagement ended, but Matthew subsequently began a relationship with another Jewish woman.

A Harmonious Blending

When we married, our two sons were twenty-three-year-old college graduates, living on their own. We have had many warm and loving family celebrations together, some involving

Barbara Miksch, "What a Blessing: My Remarriage and Our Interfaith Family." InterfaithFamily.com, 2007. Reproduced by permission.

religious holidays and others just because our sons enjoy getting together. Although they have never lived with us, or lived together as brothers, they each seem to be enjoying their first experience of having a sibling. Jim and I feel very lucky and blessed to have sons and extended families who are very accepting of our interfaith relationship. We know that this is easier because our sons are grown.

Our boys have seen us incorporate aspects of both our religions into our lives, beginning with our marriage ceremony. Even though they are at an age where they are not actively practicing their religions, each of our sons identifies with his faith heritage and each is comfortable with who he is.

Jim and I were married in Naples, Florida, where my mother lives year round and where Jim's parents coincidentally spend three months each year to escape Ohio winters. We were given excellent advice to have our wedding in a neutral setting, not a church or a synagogue, in order to set clear expectations for our families that we each intended to continue practicing our own faiths. We were very fortunate to have access to a lovely room in the high-rise my mother's lives in, where we exchanged our vows in a beautiful ceremony surrounded by our families, followed by dinner in my mother's apartment.

Although we had intended to have a rabbi and a minister participate, our experience with the rabbi was quite uncomfortable. As a result, we were married by a wonderful Presbyterian minister who embraced our unique situation, stated that he believed God had a hand in bringing us together, and even alluded during the ceremony to the fact that God must be playing a trick on us because Jews and Christians were not supposed to fall in love. He very lovingly and warmly wove Jewish and Christian elements into our ceremony, and had our sons be the witnesses who stood with him as he performed the marriage. He included readings from the Old and New Testament, the Seven Wedding Blessings, and the blessing over wine. Our sons participated by saying the blessing over wine, my son in Hebrew and Matthew in English, using a crystal Kiddish cup (wine glass) that Jim had given me for Hanukkah.

Becoming Stepbrothers

Michael and Matthew roomed together while we were in Naples, and quickly revealed how they were going to adapt to being stepbrothers in an interfaith family. I took little gift bags to their room with favorite snacks and drinks for each of them. I looked at Matthew and asked if he was ready to assume his new, awesome responsibility of becoming the older brother. I then looked at my son and said, "Sorry Michael, you are not the oldest any more." Matt asked me how far apart in age they were. I counted and told him about five-and-a-half months. Without missing a beat, Matt smiled and said, "So, technically we're twins." We had a great laugh, but we still refer to them sometimes as "the twins."

Since we were married out of town, we had a party several months later to celebrate with our friends and share some of our wedding experiences. Jim welcomed everyone and described our wedding to give them a flavor of what we had included. Then he asked the boys to give the blessing over wine. When the boys got up, Michael took the glass, recited the prayer in English and handed the wine to Matthew, who proceeded to give the blessing in Hebrew. I was totally surprised they had switched roles, but suddenly realized that when we were waiting to get up in front of our friends, the boys were joking with me about who gets to go first. "I want to go first." "No, the oldest goes first." I love how they played at being little brothers who fight and that Matthew made the effort to learn to recite the prayer in Hebrew!

Because Michael grew up in an interfaith family, he had always been accustomed to celebrating Jewish and Christian holidays. Matthew had been experiencing the same because of his relationships with Jewish women. Our current situation is a sharing of both faith practices, melding traditions from the boys' previous lives. Every holiday season has brought fun experiences: potato latkes for Hanukkah, picking out a Christmas tree to be cut down at a tree farm, and Easter baskets filled with favorite candy. Matthew has moved out of town, which means fewer holidays together, but we are looking forward to many years of shared holiday experiences in our new blended family.

A Marriage Blending Family and Race

Bill Grady

Bill Grady, who has four white and four biracial children, writes about how in his family he has not allowed race to become a defining issue. He and his wife had to confront and fight racial and family stereotypes, but he believes that societal perceptions of blended and mixed-race families have outlived their usefulness, and that his family is a living example of harmonious diversity.

My wife Kathleen was born in Leiceister, England, 100 miles north of London during World War II. Her dad was a proud member of the Grenadier Guards, the crimson clad regiment charged with the safety of the Royal Family.

At 18 she married her first husband, an African-American G.I., and took the bold step of moving to the United States. The couple eventually had four children, who were raised in the 1960s and 1970s in mostly black communities including Chicago's Altgeld Gardens housing projects.

Like mothers everywhere, Kathy sacrificed for her children as her husband attempted many different jobs before landing a career position with the Chicago Transit Authority. She became close to her in-laws, learned to cook soul food, and provide care for the family elders, while reaching back into her own "finishing school" upbringing and instilling etiquette with a British flair in her children.

Race Should Not Be Divisive

When I was young, my Irish American family moved often—living in [Chicago]'s Back of the Yards neighborhood, Ca-

Bill Grady, "Here's the Story of a Man Named Grady . . . ," *Chicago Tribune*, May 22, 2008.

naryville, and Marquette Park. Each community had an insular quality with its own reputation for being racist. I watched as some residents took pride in their divisiveness; while many others viewed it as shameful.

That's how I began to realize that one size doesn't fit all where race is concerned. People are individuals. Stereotypes often get in the way of seeing that. Like Kathy, I married my first wife when I was young. We also had four wonderful children.

Recently divorced, Kathy and I met in the early 1980s and fell in love. We decided to marry in 1984 and were faced with all the normal challenges that accompany blending families. But with ours, there was something extra: Our family would be composed of two white parents, four white children and four biracial ones.

My children were in their early teens and lived with their mother in [suburban] Evergreen Park. But they spent alternate weekends and every Wednesday night with me.

Kathy's children were young adults. None of them lived with us initially, though many have moved in from time to time, either while attending college, returning after graduation or during furloughs from the Army.

Learning the Comfort Zone

There have been instances during which one of our eight children stepped out of his or her comfort zone to support a step-sibling. When my son Bill played basketball at Evergreen Park High School, Kathy's son Fred went to the home games to cheer him on.

As Fred was usually the only African-American in the gym at that time and quite tall, Bill's friends began calling out "Hakeem" [in reference to NBA star Hakeem Olajuwon] whenever he entered. But there were other more sobering moments. Sometimes my children were taunted or even threatened when peers realized that they had step siblings who were biracial.

We're proud to say that all of our children have been comfortable in our home, and with our neighbors. Our block in the Beverly neighborhood is composed of a racially mixed group of professionals who have lived in their homes since we moved into ours over two decades ago.

One way to combat prejudice, we've learned, is to do it with humor. Our home environment allows us to laugh and tease one another about things that others may avoid out of the fear of appearing racist.

It Takes Humor

OK, ready for these examples: We joke about how our children and grandchildren have every combination of hair possible, from the so-called "good hair" to "bad hair" to no hair. We've paid ridiculous sums of money for summer braids, French braids, and *micros*, whatever those are. We've also used flat irons to straighten hair; and perms to curl hair. (I happen to use the same $4 hand brush I've had most of my adult life. One swipe and I'm good to go.)

We also observe and openly make fun of the racial stereotypes. Blacks are always late, play basketball, eat ribs, can't swim but can dance, like rap music until age 30 when adulthood starts to set in, always expect to take a plate home at a get-together, and think they're styling when their red shoes and hat match their red suit.

Whites are short, slow, naïve about the ways of the world, drink wine instead of beer, are afraid of all blacks, like rock music before age 30, and country & western music after that, eat their steak rare, learn to say "cool" before saying mama, love camping, and perform karaoke on Tuesday nights.

We laugh together because we realize that *absolutely* none of this is *absolutely* true.

Kathy and I now have 22 grandchildren and another on the way. More than half of them are biracial. It's important to note that we are not saints who just love everybody. That would be boring. What we are, however, are people who wait to know more about you before we form an opinion. And we never expect you to be just like us.

Kathy and I are raising two biracial, teenaged granddaughters. I don't allow their friends to wear do-rags in my house and we believe adolescents should be supervised. Beyond that, it's a crapshoot regarding whether you'll hear the music of Willie Nelson or Mary J. Blige when you enter our home.

I deeply understand that one of the traits that separates humans from lower level animals is our ability to think and make decisions, and those decisions are the product of emotions and past experiences. It's normal to be drawn toward others like ourselves. Our hope for the world is that people at least be open to an attraction to those who are different.

Organizations to Contact

The editors have compiled the following list of organizations concerned with the issues debated in this book. The descriptions are derived from materials provided by the organizations. All have publications or information available for interested readers. The list was compiled on the date of publication of the present volume; the information provided here may change. Be aware that many organizations take several weeks or longer to respond to inquiries, so allow as much time as possible.

American Blended Family Association (ABFA)
Washington, DC
(202) 527-9407
e-mail: info@usabfa.org
Web site: www.usabfa.org

ABFA is a not-for-profit membership organization of blended families and stepfamilies dedicated to addressing the needs and interests of more than 100 million Americans. It is funded by members and works to enable families to have educational, legal, and professional resources available in their lives in order to benefit themselves, their families, and society. Articles and press releases can be accessed on its Web site.

Bonus Families
4713 First Street, Suite 115, Pleasanton, CA 94566
Web site: www.bonusfamilies.com

Bonus Families is trying to change the way society looks at coparenting after divorce or separation. Its goal is to offer mediation, conflict management, support, and education to people attempting to combine families. Articles are available on its Web site.

National Center for Fathering
PO Box 413888, Kansas City, MO 64141
(800) 593-DADS
Web site: www.fathers.com

The National Center for Fathering is a nonprofit organization. Its Web site provides free resources for dads in nearly every fathering situation, including new dads and granddads, divorced dads and stepfathers, adoptive dads and father figures. The center also airs a daily radio program; selected programs can be downloaded from the Web site as podcasts.

The National Stepfamily Resource Center (NSRC)
e-mail: stepfamily@auburn.edu
Web site: www.stepfamilies.info

The NSRC is a division of Auburn University's Center for Children, Youth, and Families (CCYF). Its primary objective is serving as a clearinghouse of information, linking family science research on stepfamilies, and best practices in work with couples and children in stepfamilies. It publishes facts and FAQs about stepfamilies, posts research summaries and annotated bibliographies of stepfamily research, and develops educational materials for use with stepfamilies.

Stepfamily Foundation
333 West End Ave., New York, NY 10023
(212) 877-3244 • fax: (212) 362-7030
e-mail: stepfamily@aol.com
Web site: www.stepfamily.org

The foundation's mission is to assist stepfamilies in making relationships that function well. It addresses issues of how to organize a stepfamily, how to build a partnership, roles, rules, responsibilities, manners, discipline, and more. The foundation's work is supported by substantial research involving more than three thousand people. Articles are offered on its Web site.

Stepfamily Foundation of Alberta

Suite 201, 4803 Centre Street NW, Calgary, AB
T2E 2Z6
Canada
(403) 245-5744 • fax: (403) 228-4270
e-mail: info@stepfamily.ca
Web site: www.stepfamily.ca

The Stepfamily Foundation of Alberta is a not-for-profit organization that focuses exclusively upon the concerns and needs of stepfamilies. It seeks to prevent stepfamily breakdown by providing services to address and resolve the difficulties that are characteristic of the stepfamily experience. Articles and Web links are available on its Web site.

For Further Research

Books

Paul Amato and Alan Booth, *A Generation at Risk: Growing Up in an Era of Family Upheaval*. Cambridge, MA: Harvard University Press, 2000.

Elizabeth Church, *Understanding Stepmothers: Women Share Their Struggles, Successes and Insights*. Scarborough, ON: HarperCollins Canada, 2004.

Genevieve Clapp, *Divorce and New Beginnings: A Complete Guide to Recovery, Solo Parenting, Co-parenting, and Stepfamilies*. Hoboken, NJ: Wiley, 2000.

Valerie Coleman, *Blended Families: An Anthology*. Dayton, OH: Pen of the Writer, 2006.

Jacquelyn B. Fletcher, *A Career Girl's Guide to Becoming a Stepmom*. New York: HarperCollins, 2007.

Sarah Harper, *Families in Ageing Societies: A Multi-Disciplinary Approach*. New York: Oxford University Press, 2004.

Margaret Howden, *Making Molehills Out of Mountains: A Practical Guide for Stepfamilies*. Clifton Hill, Victoria, Australia: Stepfamily Association of Victoria, 2004.

Patricia Kelley, *Developing Healthy Stepfamilies: Twenty Families Tell Their Stories*. Binghamton, NY: Haworth Press, 2003.

Arthur Kornhaber, *The Grandparent Solution: How Parents Can Build a Family Team for Practical, Emotional, and Financial Success*. Hoboken, NJ: Jossey-Bass, 2004.

Barbara LeBey, *Remarried with Children: Ten Secrets for Successfully Blending and Extending Your Family*. New York: Bantam, 2004.

Jean Lipman-Bluementhal, et al., *Step Wars: Overcoming the Perils and Making Peace in Adult Stepfamilies*. New York: St. Martin's Press, 2004.

Jeanette Lofas, *Stepparenting*. New York: Citadel Press, 2004.

Elizabeth Marquardt, *Between Two Worlds: The Inner Lives of Children of Divorce*. New York: Crown, 2005.

Mary Ann Mason, Arlene Skolnick and Stephen Sugarman, *All Our Families: New Policies for a New Century*. New York: Oxford University Press, 2002.

William Pinsof and Jay Lebow, *Family Psychology: The Art of the Science*. New York: Oxford University Press, 2005.

Sonja Ridden, *Hell. . .p! I'm a Stepmother*. Camberwell, Victoria: Australian Council for Educational Research, 2002.

Elizabeth Seddon, *Creative Parenting After Separation*. Crows Nest, Australia: Allen & Unwin, 2003.

Chris Segrin and Jeanne Flora, *Family Communication*. Philadelphia: Lawrence Erlbaum Associates, 2005.

Gordon Taylor and Carri Taylor, *Stepfamilies: Bringing the Pieces to Peace*. Oklahoma City: Opportunities Unlimited, 2003.

Edward Teyber, *Helping Children Cope with Divorce*. Hoboken, NJ: Jossey-Bass, 2001.

Anita L. Vangelisti, *Handbook of Family Communication*. Philadelphia: Lawrence Erlbaum Associates, 2004.

Judith Wallerstein, Julia Lewis, and Sandra Blakeslee, *The Unexpected Legacy of Divorce: The 25 Year Landmark Study*. New York: Hyperion, 2000.

Froma Walsh, *Normal Family Processes: Growing Diversity and Complexity*. New York: Guilford Press, 2003.

Susan Wisdom and Jennifer Green, *Stepcoupling: Creating and Sustaining a Strong Marriage in Today's Blended Family*. New York: Three Rivers Press, 2002.

Periodicals

Julie E. Artis, "Maternal Cohabitation and Child Well-Being Among Kindergarten Children," *Journal of Marriage and Family*, vol. 69, 2007.

Dawn Braithwaite, M. Chad Mcbride, and Paul Schrodt, "'Parent Teams' and the Everyday Interactions of Co-parenting in Stepfamilies," *Communication Reports*, June 22, 2003.

Claire Cartwright, "Stepfamily Living and Parent-Child Relationships: An Exploratory Investigation," *Journal of Family Studies*, October 2005.

Claire Cartwright and F. Seymour, "Young Adults' Perceptions of Parents' Responses in Stepfamilies: What Hurts? What Helps?" *Journal of Divorce & Remarriage*, vol. 38, 2002.

G.J. Cohen, "Helping Children and Families Deal with Divorce and Separation," *Pediatrics*, November 2002.

Lisa Cohn, "Workin' Out: Feeling the Burn as Stepfamilies Help You Stretch—Emotionally," *Your Stepfamily Magazine*, March–April 2003.

Kimberly Davis, "Making Blended Families Work," *Ebony*, October 2000.

Natalie Gately, Lisbeth Pike, and Paul Murphy, "An Exploration of the Impact of the Family Court Process on 'Invisible' Stepparents," *Journal of Divorce & Remarriage*, vol. 44, 2006.

I. Gerrard, "Disenfranchised Grief in Stepfamilies," *Grief Matters*, Autumn 2002.

Brian Higginbotham, "Making Adult Stepfamilies Work: Strategies for the Whole Family When a Parent Marries Later in Life," *Journal of Comparative Family Studies*, vol. 37, 2006.

Jonathan Kelley and M.D.R. Evans, "Stepparenting in Australia," *Australian Social Monitor*, March 2003.

Valarie King, "When Children Have Two Mothers: Relationships with Nonresident Mothers, Stepmothers, and Fathers," *Journal of Marriage and Family*, December 2007.

Kathleen A. Lamb, "'I Want to Be Just Like Their Real Dad'—Factors Associated with Stepfather Adoption," *Journal of Family Issues*, September 2007.

Gary Marks, "Family Size, Family Type and Student Achievement: Cross-National Differences and the Role of Socioeconomic and School Factors," *Journal of Comparative Family Studies*, Winter 2006.

S. Martin, "Commitment and Cohabitation with Stepfamilies," *Threshold*, April 2003.

Mary Ann Mason et al., "Stepparents: De Facto Parents, Legal Strangers," *Journal of Family Issues*, vol. 23, no. 4, 2002.

Sheryl Nance-Nash, "Managing a Blended Family: Crafting a Financial Plan for Two Families That Merge Through Marriage Is Serious Business. Here's How to Do It Right," *Black Enterprise*, February 2004.

Lixia Qu and Ruth Weston, "Snapshot of Couple Families with Stepparent-Child Relationships," *Family Matters*, Autumn 2005.

Marjorie Smith, "Relationships of Children in Stepfamilies with Their Non-resident Fathers," *Family Matters*, Autumn 2004.

Rebecca Speer and April Trees, "The Push and Pull of Stepfamily Life: The Contribution of Stepchildren's Autonomy and Connection-Seeking Behaviors to Role Development in Stepfamilies," *Communication Studies*, vol. 58, no. 4, 2007.

Index

A

Abandonment feelings, 31–35, 41–47
ABFA (American Blended Family Association), 12, 14
Adjustment process for stepfamilies, 50–58, 68–69
    See also Stepchildren; Stepfamilies; Stepfathers; Stepmothers
Adoption, 46–47
Adultery, 27–28, 41, 42
African Americans, 13
    See also Multiracial families
Ahrons, Constance, 81
Alcohol abuse, 28–29
American Blended Family Association (ABFA), 12, 14
American Psychological Association, 58
Arguments. *See* Fighting and arguments; Tension

B

Belonging, 73–76, 77
Blended families
    as fantasy, 49–50
    including ex-spouses, 59–63, 81–85
    multiracial families, 73–76
    religion and, 25–28, 36–40, 86–89
    stress and, 14, 24–30
Bligh, Captain, 31, 33
Brady Bunch (TV show)
    as example of blended family, 13, 14, 18
    as setting false expectations, 55, 56
    social acceptance of divorce and, 13
Brown, Dave, 33
Brown, Len, 33

C

Careb, Duane, 49
Child molestation, 33–34
Children of divorced families
    abandonment feelings, 31–35, 41–47
    deterioration of relationship with father, 39–40, 43–44
    parents dating and, 44–45, 51, 57
    remarriage of parents and, 51
    See also Stepchildren; Stepfathers; Stepmothers
Christian, Brenda, 31
Christian, Dennis, 33
Christian, Fletcher, 31
Christian, Randy, 33
Christian, Steve, 33
Church of England, 42
Cohn, Lisa, 59–63
Communal living, 77–84
Cooking, 18, 22–23, 29
"Crock pot stepfamilies," 50
Cultural lag, 84–85

D

Dating (parents), 44–45, 51, 57
Deal, Ron, 49–54

Detachment, 52
Diversity, 73–76, 90–93
Divorce
absent father and, 31–35, 41–47
ex-spouses included in blended family, 59–63, 81–85
Father's Day and, 36–40
group marriage and, 79–80
negative experience of children, 24, 27–30
rejection feelings of stepparents and, 57
statistics, 70
Divorce rates, 12
Divorced Families (Ahrons), 81

E

Economics, 17–20
Education and school, 14, 66, 73–76
Esplin, Kathryn, 24–30
Ex-spouses, 59–63, 81–85

F

Family economics, 17–20
Father's Day, 36–40
Fighting and arguments, 24–25, 59
See also Tension
Forgiveness, 53
Franczak, Margaret, 13
Friedman, Lyssa, 17–20
Fronczak, Norbert, 13
Future Shock (Toffler), 78

G

Gibson, Mel, 31
Ginther, Donna, 14
Good Divorce (Ahrons), 81
Grady, Bill, 90–93
Group marriage, 77–84
Growthtrac, 49

H

Hanson, Laurie McGough, 67–71
Harrison, Laird, 77–84
Holmes, Derrick, 42
Holmes, Kelly, 41–42, 44
Homeschooling, 73

I

Institute for Family Research and Education, 13
Interfaith marriages, 86–89
Interracial families, 73–76
Ivens, Sarah, 41

J

Jewish families, 36–40, 86–89

K

Kaeck, Daniel, 13
Kingsolver, Barbara, 12, 14

L

Lupton, Michelle, 31–35
Lynott, Marc, 36–40

M

Mack, Heidi Bernadesse, 21–23
McClenon, Jennifer Busse, 55–58
Merkel, William, 59
Miller, Dawn, 64–66
Molestation, 33–34
Mormon families, 25–28

Mother's Day, 64–66
Mueller, Jim, 49
Multiracial families, 73–76
MultiracialSky.com, 73–76

N

Normality concept, 75

O

One Family, Two Family, New Family: Stories and Advice for Stepfamilies (Cohn and Merkel), 59
Open Letter to the 2008 (Presidential) Candidates (ABFA), 12

P

Partridge, Don, 13–14
Partridge, Jenetha, 13–14
Patience, 52
Pitcairn Island, 31–35
Poland, 24, 29
Pollak, Robert, 14
Polyamory, 78
Presbyterian families, 86–89

R

Rage, 37
Rape, 33
Religion
    Jewish families, 36–40, 86–89
    Mormon families, 25–28
    Presbyterian families, 86–89
Remarriage of divorced parents, 51, 70, 79, 86–89

S

School and education, 14, 66, 73
Sibling bonding
    positive experiences of stepchildren, 17–20
Sims, Sandy, 13
Single-parent families, 42–43
Smart Stepfamily (Deal), 49
Snell, Dan, 14, 15
Stepchildren
    ex-spouses and, 59–63, 81–85
    group marriage and, 77–84
    illnesses and, 69
    interfaith families and, 86–89
    multiracial families and, 90–93
    negative experiences with stepmothers, 24–30
    positive experiences in sibling bonding, 17–20
    positive experiences with stepfathers, 36–47
    positive experiences with stepmothers, 21–23
Stepfamilies
    blended family as fantasy, 49–50
    "crock pot stepfamilies," 50
    including ex-spouses, 54–63, 59–63, 81–85
    interfaith families and, 86–89
    multiracial families and, 73–76
    prevalence of, 13, 49
    religion and, 25–28, 36–40, 86–89
    time for adjustment and, 50–52, 68–69
Stepfamily Association of America's Advisory Council, 49

Stepfathers
adjustment process, 50–54
adoption of stepchildren, 46–47
Father's Day and, 36–40
multiracial families and, 90–93
positive experiences of stepchildren with, 36–47
Stepmothers
adjustment process, 50–58, 68–69
detachment and, 52, 57–58
Mother's Day and, 64–66
multiracial families and, 90–93
negative experiences of stepchildren with, 24–30
positive experiences of stepchildren with, 21–23
stepchildren's illnesses and, 69
Stereotyping, 73–76, 92–93
Stress, 14, 24–30

T

Tension, 24–30, 37–38
See also Fighting and arguments
TheStepfamilyLife.com, 64
Time factor in adjustment for stepfamilies, 50–52, 68–69
Toffler, Alvin, 77

U

Uintas Wilderness, 77
U.S. Department of Health and Human Services, 12

W

Weddings, 7, 47, 68, 70, 86–89